Basic Projects and Plantings for the Garden

Basic Projects and Plantings for the Garden

Tim Morehouse

Illustrations by Frank Clark
Photographs by Ezra Haggard

STACKPOLE BOOKS

Copyright © 1993 by Stackpole Books

Published by
STACKPOLE BOOKS
Cameron and Kelker Streets
P.O. Box 1831
Harrisburg, PA 17105

All rights reserved, including the right to reproduce this book or portions thereof in any form or by any means, electronic or mechanical, including photocopying, recording, or by any information storage and retrieval system, without permission in writing from the publisher. All inquiries should be addressed to Stackpole Books, Cameron and Kelker Streets, P.O. Box 1831, Harrisburg, Pennsylvania 17105.

Printed in the United States of America

First Edition

10 9 8 7 6 5 4 3 2 1

Cover photo by Ezra Haggard
Cover design by Tracy Patterson

Portions of this work have been reprinted with permission from "Make Your Own Flagstones for a Woodland Retreat," March 1990, *Green Scene*; "A Tiny Pool," August/September 1988, *Flower & Garden*; and *Victorian Homes*.

Library of Congress Cataloging-in-Publication Data

Morehouse, Tim.
    Basic projects and plantings for the garden / Tim Morehouse ; illustrations by Frank Clark ; photographs by Ezra Haggard. — 1st ed.
      p.   cm.
    ISBN 0–8117–3048–4 : $9.95
    1. Garden structures—Design and construction. 2. Landscape gardening. I. Title.
TH4961.M66 1993
717—dc20
                                              92-30915
                                                 CIP

For Sarah Elizabeth, Rebecca, and Emily: three little women in whose minds dwell all sweet thoughts and harmonies
— Tim

For Ruby Clark, a terrific iris gardener who taught me the value of patience, beauty, and horse manure,
and
Francis J. Clark, Jr., the most self-reliant man I've ever known, whose craftsman's hand is evident in my work
— Frank

For all my clients who made this book possible, especially Ceci Perry and Tim Johnson
— Ezra

Contents

Acknowledgments viii
Foreword ix
Introduction xii

STONE & BRICK PROJECTS

1. Brick and Stone Edging 3
2. Brick and Stone Paths 10
3. More Brick Designs: Terrace, Gutter Run-Off, Landing 15
4. Dry Stone Streambed 23

PLANT SUPPORTS

5. Wire Supports for Climbers 29
6. Attached Rose Support 34
7. Wooden Free-Form Arched Trellis 38
8. Wooden Enclosed Arched Trellis 42
9. Wooden Cage and Tripod Rose Supports 48

READY-MIX CONCRETE PROJECTS

10. Free-Form Flagstones 57
11. Miniature Reflecting Pools 61
12. Trough Gardens 67

POOLS AND FOUNTAINS

13	Informal Pool	77
14	Formal Pool	85
15	Cascading Water	89
16	Formal Fountain	92

GARDEN STRUCTURES

17	Garden Screen	97
18	Privacy Barrier	104
19	Freestanding Arbor	110
20	Formal Rose Garden with Brick Paths and Fountain	117

Sources of Supplies   125
Index   126

Acknowledgments

Acknowledgments weave together thirty-five years of gardening pleasures and include many people: Wyman Rice, a clay sculptor, built the wooden structures designed by Ezra. My sons, Seth and Eric, carried bags of peat moss, stacks of bricks, and piles of stones into my garden long before they realized that monetary rewards were their due. Apologies to Nancy for keeping Frank away from dinner while the three of us argued and debated over each chapter. Special thanks to Ceci, from whose garden many of the photographs and designs were conceived; to Jean, whose love for the old roses would rival that of the Empress Josephine; and last, to Miriam—eighty-four years young—who has forgotten more about perennials than I will ever know.

Foreword

You have brought back armloads of your favorite plants from the nursery. Now, how are you to make a garden from them? You don't belong to a garden club and haven't even gardened before, but you want a nice yard. Tim Morehouse gives you good advice about some basic garden needs here. First, put the plants aside for a while and consider the bones of your garden. Construction usually requires earth to be moved, so it makes sense to do it before putting in plants. So long as they are in a shady place and not neglected, the plants will wait until a few decisions are made about the shape of the garden and the permanent features it will contain. Look through Tim's projects for those that suit you and your lot. If there is to be lawn, will the edges need trimming, or do you prefer the ingenious brick edges that Tim suggests? Do you like the idea of roses lifted onto pillars to flower at eye level? What about a pool?

Remember, the contours of the lot, the shapes of the beds, and the directions of paths do more to determine the character of your garden than do the plants you choose. You may feel that a straight path is too severe, but there is no space for a winding one; soften the straight path by choosing a sandy surface or laying brick in an interesting pattern. You want only roses in your garden; vary their heights, with roses climbing on pillars and spread on trellises, as is done with astounding effect in the great gardens of Europe. You like to see birds in the garden; a pool will attract them and a fountain will amuse both them and you, as they fly through the spray on warm days.

Many people sketching out their first garden allow too much space for lawn. I've often wondered why this is—especially since they know it must be mowed and watered—and conclude that while grass if familiar to new gardeners, other kinds of plants are unfamiliar and their care a mystery, so too few are purchased. New gardeners also feel, I guess, that a lawn will be played on and should therefore be as large as possible. Some find that as their children grow and their love of plants increases, the lawn is whittled away to make space for flowers. Then to their surprise the garden assumes new character—the proper proportions are reached for the first time only as the lawn shrinks. For a simple garden, a good balance is about one-third grass and two-thirds flowering plants.

In large gardens problems are fewer; interest is satisfied with the variety of plants alone, and the eye is drawn into the distance, creating a sense of anticipation in vistas yet to be enjoyed. Even bald patches in the lawn are overlooked in the grand sweep of grass. But yours is a small lot, and in small gardens everything tends to be seen at a glance, and it is difficult to include sufficient variety of plants to maintain interest. In our small gardens there is no distance, and everything is seen at close quarters and must be able to survive scrutiny. In small gardens, then, variety must be introduced through structural detail and good ornament, but such structures must be well made and installed.

Pay attention, then, to the advice Tim Morehouse gives here. A few simple additions well constructed as he suggests can change a small, dull garden into one that intrigues with novelty and surprise. The gardener will find enjoyment in the projects themselves and in the possibilities they open up when completed. A pool, for example, brings to the garden not only the opportunity for fish, their movement and color, but watery sounds and reflections, too. And that is only the beginning: a completely new range of plants can be grown, some in the water, others near it. Water in a pool cools and moistens nearby air, allowing some plants to thrive as they never would in other parts of the garden.

Even so simple a device as a frame for supporting roses changes the garden in ways that may surprise you. Height provided by roses on pillars, for example, may attract birds that never stayed in your garden before. Though sparrows go anywhere in search of food and forage on the ground as long as need be, some other birds, such as flycatchers, prefer to sit above the ground searching the territory for prey, then make quick sorties to pick it up. Without perches at their preferred height these creatures pass your garden by.

And these structures are durable. Unlike plants, which are ephemeral—flowering for a week or a month each year, and succumbing to neglect—paths, steps, retaining walls, and pools remain; the quality of permanence they bring is reassuring and is what makes them so important in a garden. Despite this, little about them is found in books on gardening. A great many volumes—too many, perhaps—can be found in bookstores on garden plants, and some on garden design, but in few of them does the author roll up his sleeves, as Tim does here, to install those essential features that transform a yard full of plants into a pleasure garden.

W. George Waters, Editor
Pacific Horticulture

Introduction

Frank Clark, the illustrator of this book and a longtime friend, once asked me while strolling through the woods on my property, "Tim, where did you find those stones you've placed here?" I laughed at his question: I had made them from ready-mix concrete tinted with brown dye, digging the holes where I wanted them and then shaping the designs myself. Frank's otherwise sharp eyes had been deceived, and I was delighted. For several years, while working in this area of my garden, I had often thought about this moment. I realized that perhaps I could share some ideas with homeowners who might think their grounds lack gardening solutions or promise.

About the same time, I was successfully experimenting with raising hardy English ferns from spore. People fascinated with unusual shade plants quickly became acquisitive gardening friends who shared my enthusiasm for ferns. A chance reference to my hobby appeared in the *New York Times*, and shortly thereafter, professional garden designer and photographer Ezra Haggard appeared one spring morning. His shrewd eye for the form, shape, texture, and color of plants opened a new world to me, which he generously shares in the pages of this book.

Fine gardening is a subtle art, and the structures used within a landscape are as vital as the plants themselves. But Ezra, Frank, and I believe that novice or less obsessed gardeners—those who would prefer grabbing a spade and hammer occasionally without abandoning their jogging shoes—can improve an existing site or create a beautiful garden that becomes the envy of the neighborhood.

Gertrude Jekyll, in her book *Wood and Garden* (1899), wrote: "The size of a garden has very little to do with its merit. It is merely an accident relating to the circumstances of the owner. It is the size of his

INTRODUCTION

heart and brain and goodwill that will make his garden either delightful or dull, as the case may be, and either leave it at the monotonous dead level, or raise it . . . towards that of a work of fine art." Before attempting any of the projects outlined in this book, you should study your property, then decide how best to incorporate a new design. For example, consider adding a trellis to give vertical dimensions to your flower border. If you're tired of staring at the boat in your neighbor's driveway, build a privacy barrier.

Each chapter includes photographs and illustrations. The steps are not complicated, and one or two people can construct the projects in just a few days or several weekends. Materials and tools listed for each project can be purchased at lumber mills, hardware stores, nurseries, and stone centers. If the tools are too expensive to purchase, you can simply rent them. Keep in mind that the same materials and tools can be used to create different structures and designs. For example, the wooden strips, nails, and screws used in making several trellis patterns are similar. Remember, too, that the dimensions of the projects can be altered to fit the size of any property.

The plants mentioned in this book will flourish in a wide range of temperatures and are only suggestions; your imagination must play a major role here. First, find out which plants are indigenous to your area. That way, you'll know what plants are hardy and grow best where you live. Visiting nursery centers, studying catalogs from mail-order sources, or simply picking the brains of experienced horticulturists will add immeasurably to your gardening expertise.

The designs you choose to create are a personal reflection of your taste, and each one should provide interest throughout the year. You will soon discover that simplicity, sensitivity, and subtlety merge to form continuity. If you begin with an idea that works for your property, you can't go wrong.

T.M.

Stone & Brick Projects

1

Brick and Stone Edging

An island bed, handsomely defined by ell-shaped brick edging, is thickly planted with pachysandra and variegated dogwoods (Cornus florida *'First Lady'*). Design by Ezra Haggard.

A WELL-KNOWN ENGLISH GARDENER once said that if you want to impress visitors, you should keep your edges trimmed. I agree. But it isn't really necessary to spend hours on your hands and knees with clippers and grass shears.

Once you decide on the size and shape of your beds, you can line them with bricks or stones to form a curb. Alongside the bed, sink the bricks vertically, two-thirds below lawn level. Facing each brick, place another one flat and lengthwise to form an L shape. The upright bricks form a neat outline for the beds, and the turf-level bricks provide a surface for the lawn mower wheels, thus eliminating hand-trimming.

If you want to use fewer bricks, try variations on this pattern. You can also use stones—rough granite blocks of approximately equal size—instead of bricks. The result will be borders that are both practical and aesthetically pleasing.

Bricks are available in a wide assortment of colors and textures. If your house is brick, choose the same kind of bricks for a unified look. Matching bricks will also make your house and garden more interesting architecturally.

Consult your building supplier about the various types of bricks available; not all bricks are for exterior use. Be sure to order enough to complete the job, or you may end up with two different colors. If you buy new bricks, you'll need three-and-one-half bricks per running foot; if bricks are old, three. For an antique, weathered look, try old bricks or stones, which are sometimes available from city rehabilitation sites. Stone centers also offer a wide selection of both old and new bricks, as well as an assortment of stones. Check the Yellow Pages of your phone directory for sources.

If you choose stones that vary in size, sinking them so that the tops are level will create a more functional and satisfying design. Choose a brick or stone pattern from one of the designs illustrated.

If your edging is extensive, you will find it less expensive to order sand in bulk from a stone center. One cubic yard equals approximately 1½ tons and will cover about 600 square feet to a depth of ½ inch.

Materials

Brick or stone
Builder's sand (a 75-pound bag will cover 8 square feet to a depth of 1 inch)
Pulverized limestone
A length of 2x4

Special Tools

Rubber mallet

BRICK & STONE EDGING

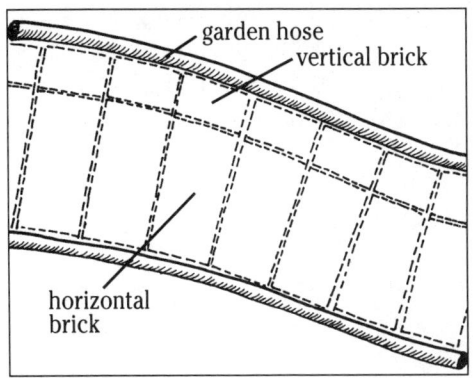

1. Stretch a garden hose (for curved lines) and string (for straight lines) to form a pattern for your edging.

2. Use a sharp straight-edge spade to remove the sod.

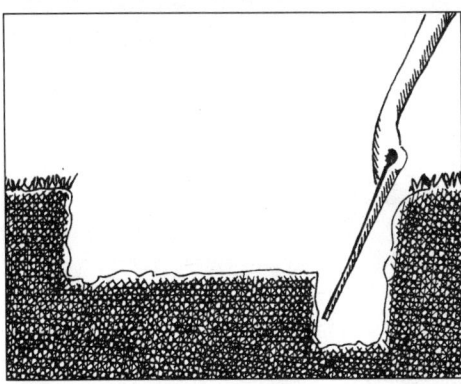

3. Cut a trench two-thirds the depth of an upright brick. Depths will vary if you are sinking stones with jagged, uneven edges.

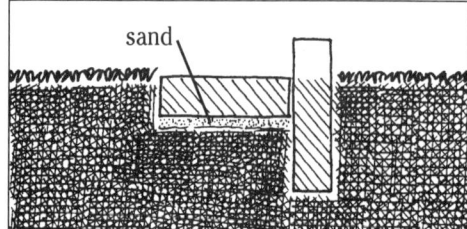

4. For easy placement of bricks, fill in the bottom of the trench with a ½-inch layer of sand.

5. Sink a single line of bricks, on end, in the trench. Tap the bricks from the side with a rubber mallet as you set them in place.

6. After laying each 3-foot length of edging, place a 2x4 on top of both horizontal and vertical surfaces, and tap with a mallet so that all bricks are level throughout the design.

7. Brush pulverized limestone into the spaces between the bricks to form a bond between the bricks and thus make the surface more secure. Using a garden hose, spray lightly with water to settle the limestone.

Suggested Plantings

For sunny locations. Plant clump-forming perennials that grow only 6 to 8 inches high and soften the edges as they sprawl. For example, the silver, felty leaves of *Stachys byzantina*, or lamb's-ears, are irresistible to the touch and beautiful with any combination of colors. I recommend *S. byzantina* 'Silver Carpet' because it doesn't bloom; the flower stalks of lamb's-ears flop after a shower and look like strips of wet mattress stuffing. This perennial spreads quickly, so plant sparingly.

The species geraniums known as cranesbills are easy to grow and produce flowers in soft, delicate shades of blue, pink, red, and white. *Geranium* 'Johnson's Blue' is a prolific bloomer for more than two months in midsummer and combines nicely with *G. sanguineum* var. striatum, a prostrate, shell-pink bloomer that performs from spring until frost. For more blues (a difficult color to find), try the dwarf campanulas such as *Campanula portenschlagiana* and *C. poscharskyana*; both are plants that will sprawl and spill over your edging, adding natural touches to your garden.

For moist, shady sites. Grow clumps of liriope (members of the lily family), ivy (especially *Hedera helix* 'Thorndale'), pachysandra, and toward the back of your bed, the taller astilbes and hostas. These plants will perform best in light, open shade. *Hosta* 'Frances Williams' is a slow grower for most gardeners (it takes several years for a clump to form), but is well worth the wait. Its leaves are a slate blue–green color with splashes of yellow, and are heavily textured, like seersucker cloth. The elegant *Hosta* 'Krossa Regal', when provided with ample water and leaf mulch, will grow into an open umbrella with lavender flowers well above the silver-blue foliage. Both of these cultivars are prize winners along the border.

Another low-grower that provides excellent texture, foliage, and flowers is *Alchemilla mollis*, or lady's-mantle. The leaves are sensational, especially when they sparkle after a heavy dew. The tiny chartreuse flowers appear in foaming clusters above the foliage and are useful in arrangements.

Don't ignore the many species of hardy ferns for moist, shady areas along the border. They are trouble-free, their fronds remain green for months, and garden pests seldom attack them. Maidenhair fern *(Adiantum pedatum)*, cinnamon fern *(Osmunda cinnamomea)*, royal fern *(Osmunda regalis)*, and Christmas fern *(Polystichum acrostichoides)* are a few of the more common ones available from garden centers and mail-order nurseries. The unfurling fronds (fiddleheads) of ferns are a distinct harbinger of spring and are beautiful in their own right.

The above-mentioned plants are only a small sampling of perennials suitable for brick and stone edging around your flower beds. Check with

The subtle mingling of soft colors and textures in Russian sage, Potentilla *'Miss Wilmott', and a globe-shaped blue spruce complements the stone edging selected to blend with the walls of the house.* Design by Ezra Haggard.

local nurseries for additional plants. As you design your plantings, keep in mind the color of your brick; a bright pink brick will clash with orange flowers, and vice versa. Stone requires more work and is often more expensive to install, but it combines easily with plants of any color.

2

Brick and Stone Paths

ALL GARDENS NEED TRANSITIONS from one area to another; attractive walks made of brick or stone serve this purpose. Paths not only form the backbone of your landscape, they also help display the best your garden has to offer. For example, curves within your paths will entice the viewer and will set off the sculptural effects created by your plantings. A walkway that curves or meanders is especially effective if it leads to a focal point, such as a specimen tree, an arbor, or a pool.

But above all, paths must be practical. If emergency runs to the herb

---

A path constructed of used brick gently curves from the driveway and leads into the garden. Planted along the edges are clumps of evergreen candytuft and herbaceous peonies. Design by Ezra Haggard.

garden are common in your household, a straight path makes more sense than a curved one. Also, keep in mind that paths should follow the contours of your property. In some cases, curves are best suited to the lay of the land; in others, straight lines are called for.

How wide should you make your paths? Again, it depends on their use. As a general rule, two people can easily stroll down a garden path 4 or 5 feet wide; one person needs 2 to 3 feet. Figure four-and-a-half bricks per square foot of walkway. This number depends on the size of the bricks; old bricks are sometimes larger than new ones.

Your walks are a permanent framework that shapes the overall design of your garden, and should be both useful and attractive. Take time to plan them carefully, and be selective about the materials you use.

Materials
Brick or stone
Builder's sand
Pulverized limestone

Special Tools
Rubber mallet
Cold chisel
Mason's chisel
Circular power saw with masonry blade
Safety glasses

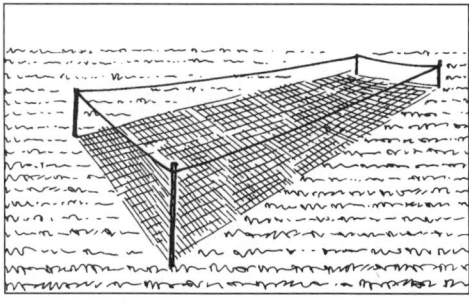

1. Outline the path, using string and stakes for a straight line and a garden hose for curves.

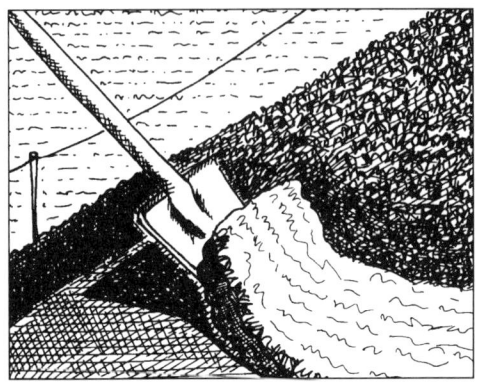

2. Dig out the sod and soil 5 inches deep. If the area tends to be soggy in winter, you may want to excavate more soil and add additional sand to your base to provide for adequate drainage.

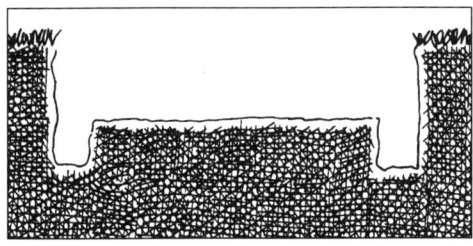

3. Along each side of the path, dig a trench two–thirds the depth of a vertical brick.

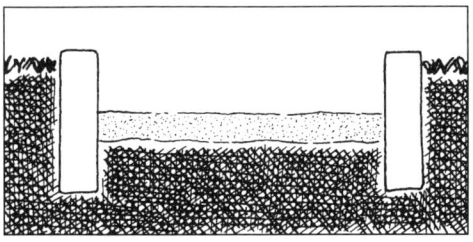

4. Position the vertical bricks, then spread sand 3 inches deep over the path. Rake it level.

5. Place the brick or stone pavers on your sand base (a basket weave pattern is illustrated), then tap the surface with a mallet and 2x4. Stand back occasionally and look at the result. In some cases, you may need more sand.

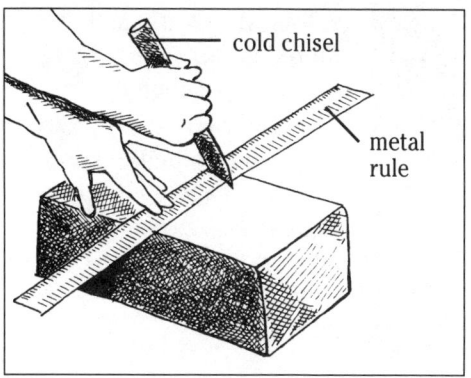

6. If you need to cut the bricks, score them with a cold chisel.

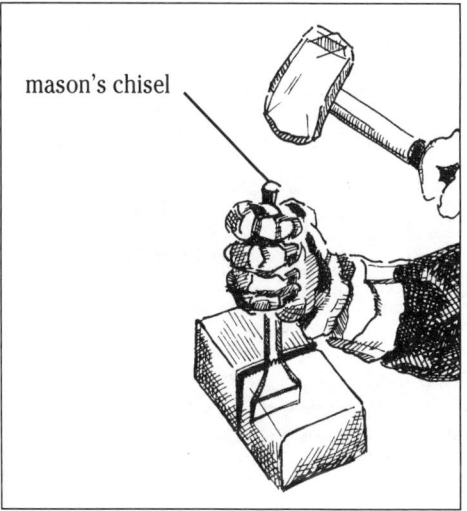

7. Place a mason's chisel on the score line and strike with a hammer to obtain a clean cut. (Always wear safety glasses when cutting or drilling brick or stone.)

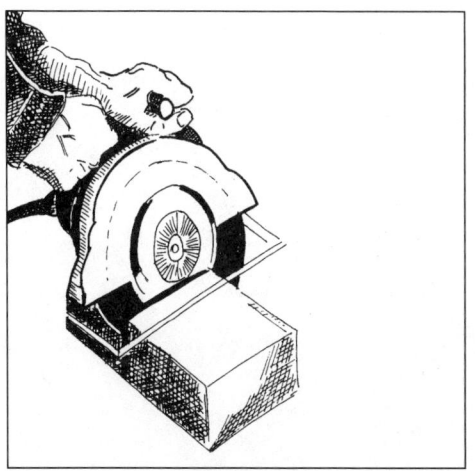

8. Another method of cutting bricks is to use a circular power saw with a masonry blade.

9. Sweep pulverized limestone on top of your bricks or stones to fill in the crevices. Settle the material into place by lightly spraying it with a garden hose. Repeat as necessary.

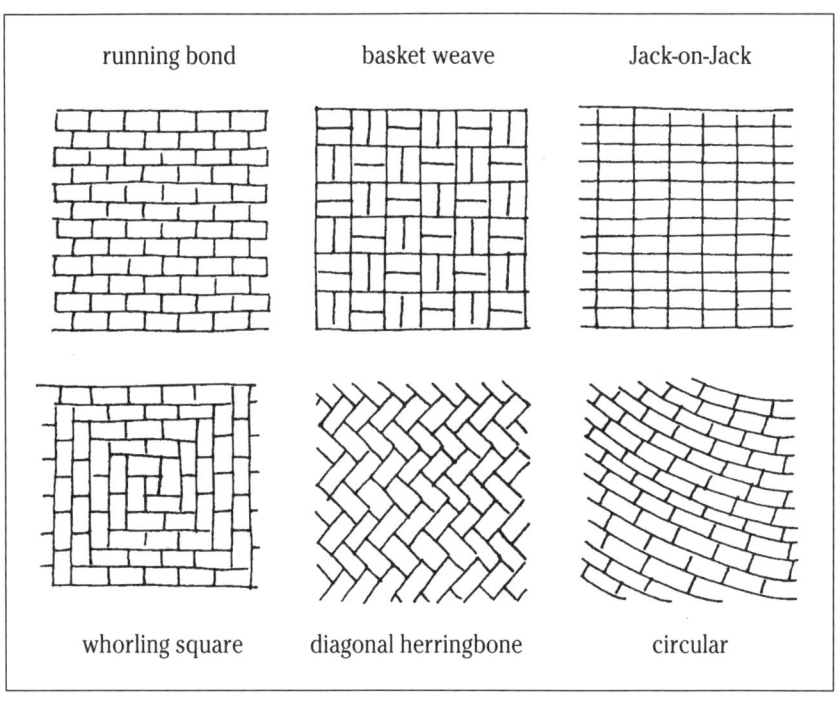

Additional brick patterns.

More Brick Designs: Terrace, Gutter Run-Off, Landing

THE USUAL SITE for a terrace is adjacent to the house. Before laying a terrace, however, check the sun's movement. Do you want exposure most of the day or part of the day? If your house is shaded by large trees but you want sunlight, it may be necessary to build your terrace away from the house and link the two with a path. Remember, too, that the angle of the sun (and thus the shadows of trees and buildings) changes through the seasons.

The size of your terrace will depend on its use. If you want to use the area for eating, consider the size of your family. Will you be entertaining friends, too? Generally, the minimum size for a terrace is 12 feet square,

---

A brick terrace in a basket-weave design provides a shaded outdoor space for entertaining. Design by Ezra Haggard.

but there is no rule for shape. Also, keep in mind the scale of your entire garden. Once you decide on location and size, choose the same materials for paving the terrace that you have used for paths in other parts of the landscape.

A gutter run–off may be necessary for directing rain water away from the terrace or house foundation. It serves a very practical function in garden design. The same is true of a stair landing. By expanding the exit and entrance area at the bottom of a flight of steps, the lawn is free of bare patches.

Terraces, gutter run-offs, and stairway landings all employ the same methods used in the construction of paths. Occasionally, curved areas will require cutting, depending on the design. As construction progresses, stand back occasionally and look at the bricks; some may need more or less sand to make the surface level.

Materials

Brick
1 cubic yard of builder's sand (order from a stone center)
Pulverized limestone

Special Tools

Rubber mallet
Cold chisel
Mason's chisel
Circular power saw with masonry blade

Terrace

1. Divide your area into sections of equal widths and lengths. Using stakes and string, outline the space.

2. Dig out the entire area so that the base will accommodate a 2-inch layer of sand under the bricks, raising them to turf level.

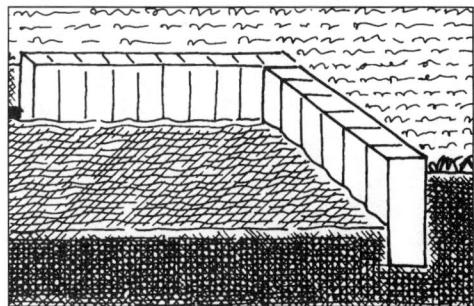

3. Dig a trench around the perimeter for vertical bricks, and place them along one side and one end of the terrace site. After the vertical bricks are in place, add a 2-inch layer of sand, then level it.

4. Lay bricks one section at a time. Use a 2x4 and a mallet to tap them securely in place. Stand back occasionally and look at the result. Add sand as needed to make the surface level.

5. Sweep pulverized limestone between the cracks and spray lightly with a garden hose.

A sloped gutter run-off from a screened summer room located near the terrace effectively channels water away from the foundation. Design by Ezra Haggard.

Gutter Run-Off

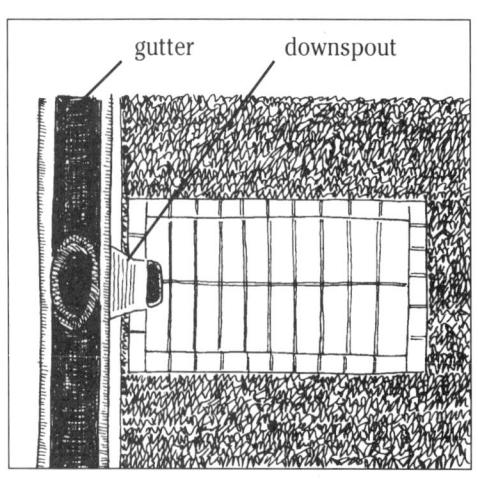

1. Lay bricks on the ground under the downspout to determine the size of your excavation. An ideal size is 3 feet long by 22 inches wide.

MORE BRICK DESIGNS

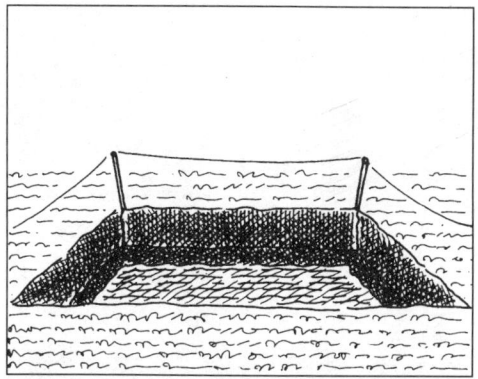

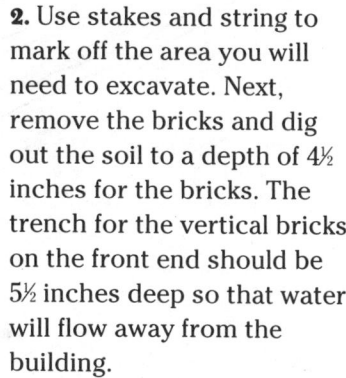

2. Use stakes and string to mark off the area you will need to excavate. Next, remove the bricks and dig out the soil to a depth of 4½ inches for the bricks. The trench for the vertical bricks on the front end should be 5½ inches deep so that water will flow away from the building.

3. Use a 2x4 and a rubber mallet to tap the vertical bricks into place on all sides.

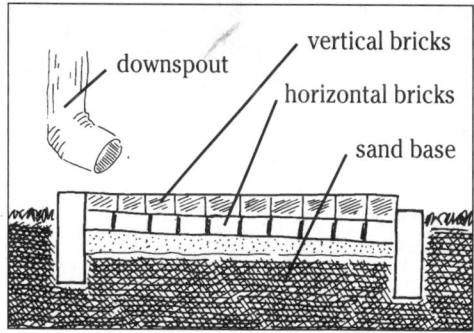

4. After the vertical edging is in place, add a sand base and grade it so that it slopes away from the house. Lay horizontal bricks on the sand base, then tap them into place with a 2x4 and a mallet. Sweep pulverized limestone between the crevices and spray lightly with a garden hose.

An elegantly curved brick landing at the base of steps leads from the pool area and is framed on each side with weeping cherries (Prunus subhirtella *'Pendula'*). Design by Ezra Haggard.

Landing

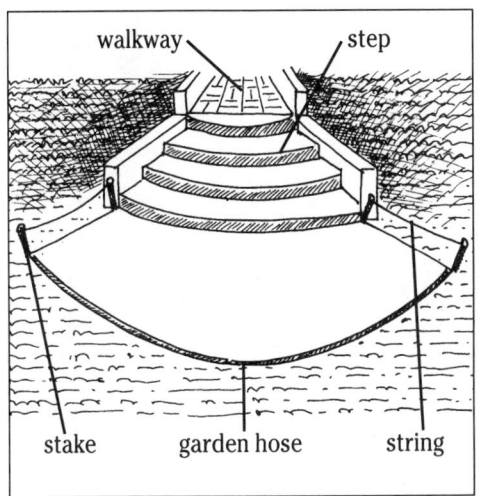

1. Mark the area for the landing with stakes, string, and a garden hose.

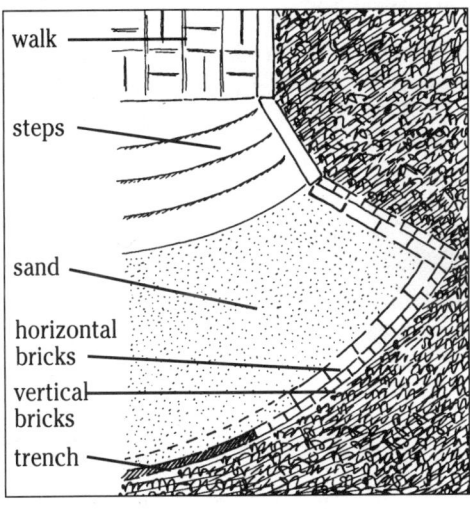

2. Dig a trench around the perimeter and insert the vertical bricks at ground level. Dig out the remaining area to a depth of 4 inches. Spread a 2-inch layer of sand over the entire area. For the inside edging, place a row of bricks horizontally at ground level next to the vertical bricks.

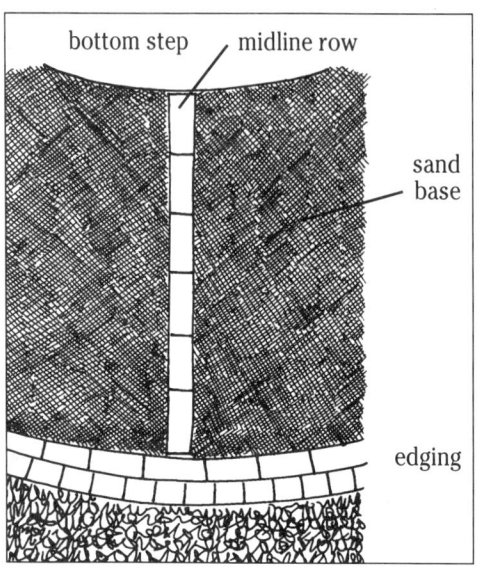

3. Place a row of horizontal bricks along the midline of the design to provide a backbone for a running bond pattern.

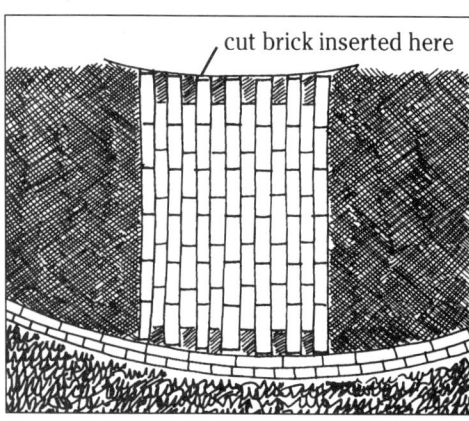

4. Lay down several rows of bricks to determine which end bricks will need to be cut to create the running bond pattern as illustrated.

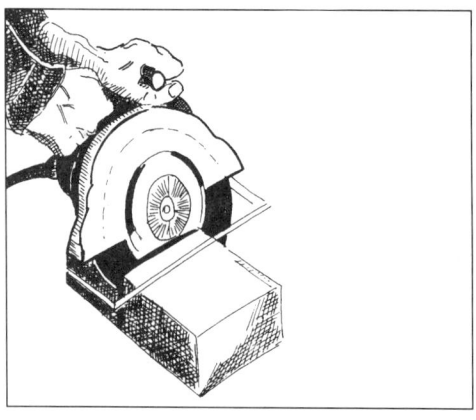

5. Use a circular power saw with a masonry blade to cut bricks needed to fill the spaces within the design. Use a 2x4 and a mallet to tap the bricks securely in place. Stand back occasionally and look at the result. Sweep pulverized limestone between the cracks and spray lightly with a garden hose.

4

Dry Stone Streambed

A dry stone streambed meanders through Asiatic and Oriental lilies, zinnias, and old-fashioned hollyhocks. The river stones are roughly the size of goose eggs. Design by Ezra Haggard.

Perhaps you have a problem spot on your property where nothing seems to flourish. Such an area is often dry and barren, the result of excess rubble left by builders. You can make these eyesores attractive, however, by constructing a dry streambed and adorning it with traditional perennials or drought-tolerant plants.

You don't have to emulate a Japanese design for this project; the dry streambed described below is simply a practical solution for a problem site. When rain falls, it will solve the problem of run-off and drainage. Such a streambed, with its graceful curves, can also serve as a walkway to other areas of the garden.

Two people can easily construct a dry stone streambed in a day. Planting the surrounding area with perennials, shrubs, bulbs, and grasses will enhance its beauty and may even make it the focal point of your landscape.

Materials
Large river stones (available at stone centers)

Special Tools
Rubber mallet

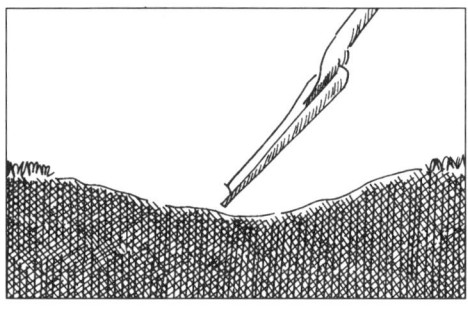

1. Remove any existing weeds or sod by scooping out the area with a shovel, then rake the path into the desired dimension and shape. If you like, you can make one end of the bed narrower to enhance the illusion of distance. Curve each side of the bed slightly upward.

2. Use a rubber mallet to tap the stones into place. Don't use a hammer; it will chip the stones.

3. Partially bury each stone, keeping the surfaces of adjoining stones reasonably even. The bed should have the overall effect of closely packed cobbles.

Suggested Plantings

For hot, sunny areas. Consider planting liriope, asters, chrysanthemums, Asiatic and Oriental lilies *(Lilium)*, several small shrubs, a dwarf holly, an assortment of herbs, and several clumps of grasses. Of course, your plantings will depend on the space around your streambed as well as other design features in the garden.

Liriope is often used as a ground cover, but when planted in clumps along a dry streambed, it will form soft mounds of strap–like arching leaves less than a foot tall. There are several cultivars with yellow variegated foliage. The flowers, which appear in late summer, are pale lavender or white.

Dwarf asters *(Aster novi-belgii)* are readily available at garden centers or from mail-order nurseries. They provide a wide range of pastel and hot colors from July through September and bloom after the lilies fade but before the chrysanthemums appear.

Asiatic lilies open in June and July; Orientals, from July through August. Asiatic and Aurelian hybrids come in a wide range of colors: nasturtium-red, gold, yellow, pink, lavender, and white. These grow about 2 feet tall and need no staking. Oriental hybrids are taller and should be staggered in clumps among other lower–growing perennials.

Near the end of your dry streambed, plant some Oriental grasses: maiden grass *(Miscanthus sinensis* 'Gracillimus') or rosy fountain grass *(Pennisetum alopecuroides)* are perfect. These grasses provide height and grace while offering interest throughout the seasons. Different striped varieties, such as Japanese silver grass, are plentiful at good garden centers. The more compact, dwarf grasses are striking along the sides of your streambed or at the foot of taller plants such as the lilies. Good choices include *Carex conica* 'Hime Kansuge', or *C. morrowii* 'Fisher's Form'.

Grasses are hardy in most regions of the country. They require little care, except for some hand grooming in the spring to remove winterkill. Always plant or divide grasses in the spring.

For dry, shady locations. Try planting *Arum italicum* 'Pictum', which seems to reverse the seasons. It produces stunning arrow–shaped leaves and spikes of red berries in the fall, grows throughout the winter, then disappears in the spring. *Bergenia cordifolia* (of the saxifrage family) is striking when grown in clumps along a border of stones. Its glossy, leathery evergreen leaves provide textural interest, and in the winter, the upper surfaces often turn a rich mahogany. This native of Siberia will thrive almost anywhere.

Cyclamen hederifolium has ivy-shaped leaves marbled in ivory and produces tiny pink flowers in autumn. Unfortunately, this beautiful plant is difficult to grow anywhere except in the Pacific Northwest. It prefers rich humus and leaf mulch, summer shade, and winter sun.

The low-growing *Epimedium* species offer attractive leaves as well as flowers in red, yellow, apricot, and a lovely white ('Niveum'). Snowdrops and other tiny spring bulbs are also effective by a dry streambed, under the taller plants.

Iris foetidissima produces tall clumps of fan-shaped leaves. The flowers are somewhat ordinary, but the foliage creates a striking effect next to bergenia, with its rounded leaves, and the tiny arrowhead-shaped leaves of epimedium.

Mahonia aquifolium, also known as Oregon grape holly, grows about 3 feet tall and produces blue fruit shaped like tiny clusters of grapes. Depending on the severity of the winter, the glossy, dark green leaves may take on a purplish tone, a striking combination with bergenia nearby.

In the arid Southwest, it's important to select plants that require a minimum of water. Willows and birches suffer from prolonged drought, but some pines can survive. Traditional annuals will flourish if planted close to the edge of the stones and watered regularly. Santolina, rosemary, sand verbena (*Abronia* spp.), and lantana do well under hot, dry conditions; they offer bright flowers and a mixture of silver and green foliage. Succulents such as octopus agave *(Agave vilmoriniana)* and *Kalanchoe blossfeldiana* are also useful. Some ground covers survive well, such as prairie verbena *(Verbena rigida)* and Rocky Mountain zinnia *(Zinnia grandiflora)*. Check with your local nursery for suggestions, and use plants indigenous to your area.

Plant Supports

5

Wire Supports for Climbers

WIRE SUPPORTS CAN BE USED to add architectural beauty to a wall or post in the garden. They are also useful for decorating a surface that you want to conceal, such as a toolshed.

A mantle of green can be trained to grow vertically, horizontally, or in a fan shape. If your garden is small, you will have more vertical than

A climbing rose makes its way along a vertical and horizontal wire support; it will eventually form a complete arch over the porch railing. Design by Ezra Haggard.

horizontal space; covering walls with greenery is practical and will also add a soothing dimension to your landscape.

Copper wire, stretched between screw eyes, is a sturdy support for any climber you plant. You can judge the size of your wire design by the type of vine you want to grow and what you want to cover. For example, the annual morning–glory vine will grow rapidly and cover a wall in one season, then die. The perennial wisteria vine is woody and tenacious, and quickly produces tendrils that will reach under roofing shingles and into downspouts.

Four feet is the best length for stretching 6–gauge wire; five–foot lengths require 8–gauge wire. If you want a rose to cover a 10-foot post and grow across a porch framework, simply stretch wire between the screw eyes arranged in a series of 4-foot segments. Although it may take several growing seasons, the plant will eventually cover the area you want it to.

Where you plant your climbers is important. A south-facing wall is ideal for roses; a north-facing location can deprive them of much–needed sunlight. Ideally, climbers should have at least half a day of sunlight (preferably morning sun) and late-afternoon shade. When choosing a site for your wire support, always check the width of the overhanging roof to determine whether your climbers will need supplementary water during dry weather. You should also consider the wind factor: no climbing plant thrives in heavy drafts.

To prepare the planting area, dig holes at least 20 inches deep and fill the bottom half with coarse rubble or pea gravel to promote drainage. The soil mixture may vary according to the plant's requirements, but any good friable topsoil supplemented with generous quantities of sphagnum peat moss will serve most climbers.

Keep in mind that these supports are only semi-permanent; if you need to paint the wall, you can simply unscrew them and lay the vines on the ground.

Although wire supports are simple to construct, remember that you may need to spend some time maintaining the vine, depending on the type you choose to grow. For instance, a climbing rose produces lovely flowers, but must be sprayed for blackspot during the growing season. Roses must also be clipped and tied to perform at their best.

Materials

   Plastic mollies (one for each hole you drill)
   Galvanized screw eyes (two screw eyes for every 4 or 5 feet of wire)
   6– or 8–gauge copper wire

WIRE SUPPORTS FOR CLIMBERS — 31

Special Tools
Electric drill with masonry bit
Safety glasses

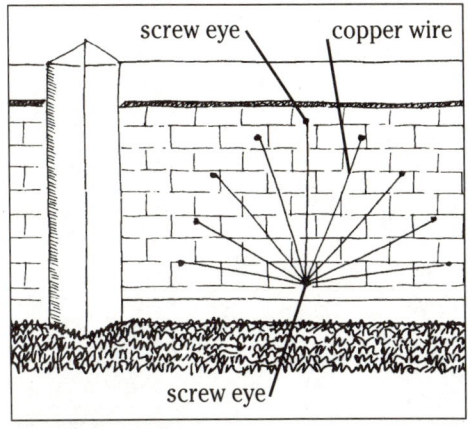

1. Mark the screw-eye pattern on the wall with chalk or pencil.

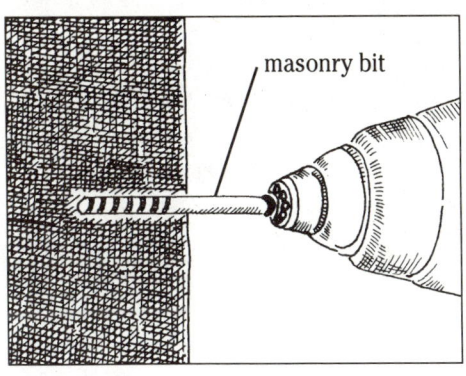

2. Using the electric drill with masonry bit, drill holes for anchors. Make the holes as wide as the mollies and ⅛ inch deeper.

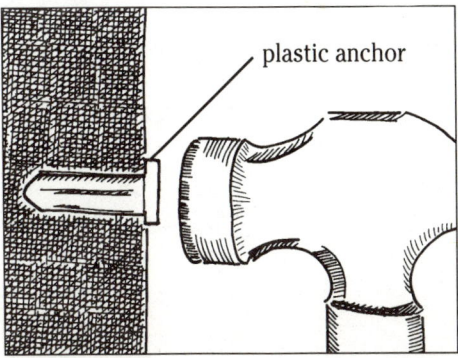

3. Tap the mollies into the holes with a hammer.

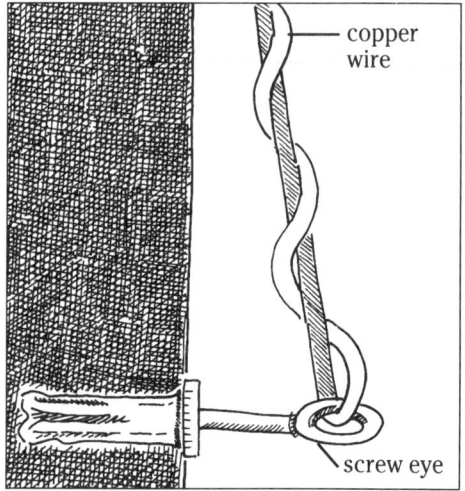

4. Insert screw eyes into the plastic mollies. Stretch the copper wire taut between the screw eyes and twist each end.

Suggested Plantings

There are basically three types of climbers: the clingers, the ramblers, and the twiners.

Clingers attach themselves to a surface by growing aerial roots. Examples of these are ivy (*Hedera* spp.), climbing hydrangea (*Hydrangea anomala* subsp. *petiolaris*), and trumpet vine (*Campsis* spp.). Clinging vines often need wire supports to start in the direction you want them to go, but they'll soon take off on their own.

The ramblers, such as climbing roses, produce long canes that must be tied into place and directed by wires as they grow. They require 8–gauge copper wire, since they tend to become heavy with age.

The twiners include sweet pea *(Lathyrus odoratus)*, morning-glory (*Ipomoea* 'Heavenly Blue'), and clematis. These vines send out lax tendrils and flourish on 6–gauge wire.

Before selecting vines, visit your local nursery to find out which grow best in your area.

The lush blooms of Rosa 'Albertine' cover a vertical wire support in a sunny corner of a walled garden. Design by Ezra Haggard.

6

Attached Rose Support

A FREE-FORM TRELLIS attached to a building is a stunning way to display roses. It not only provides a permanent covering but also adds an eye–catching vertical dimension to your wall. In both large and small gardens, a space-saving wall trellis will soon fill an empty area with rich, opulent bouquets of color and scent throughout the growing season.

Keep in mind that an attached trellis permits sun and light to enter from one side only. Roses prefer full sunlight, but some will grow and bloom in partial shade if they receive morning or afternoon sun.

The wood rose support blends with the house siding and displays Rosa 'Yellow Rambler' and 'Madame Alfred Carrière' at their best. A topiary shrub and perennials create a perfect contrast of shapes and textures at the base of the roses. Design by Ezra Haggard.

ATTACHED ROSE SUPPORT

Choose your roses carefully. Red, white, or yellow roses blend well with a pink brick wall, but a pink rose may look washed out, and orange or rust flowers will clash. If your brick is yellow, consider planting red or pink roses with glossy foliage. If your house is stone, you are lucky; any color will enhance the beauty of the wall. If your house has wood siding, you'll need to dismantle the trellis when it's time to paint. Simply unscrew the structure, pull it away from the house, and lay trellis and vine on the ground.

The instructions that follow are for building one attached rose trellis, 8 feet by 8 feet.

Materials

1x1–inch strips of pressure-treated wood measuring 8 feet long (the number of strips needed depends on the width of your siding)
Size 6D nails
Galvanized 2-inch screws

Special Tools

Electric drill
Tape rule
Safety glasses

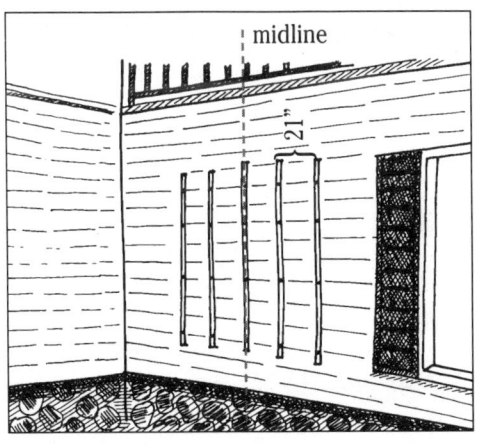

1. Using a tape rule and pencil, locate and mark the vertical midline of the area where you want the trellis. Place these marks at the top and at the bottom, 1 foot from ground level. Attach the midline vertical strip with two screws at several points. Screw the remaining verticals into place, 21 inches apart.

2. Nail the horizontal strips onto the vertical strips. If you have siding on your house, the bottom of each horizontal strip should align with the bottom of a siding panel.

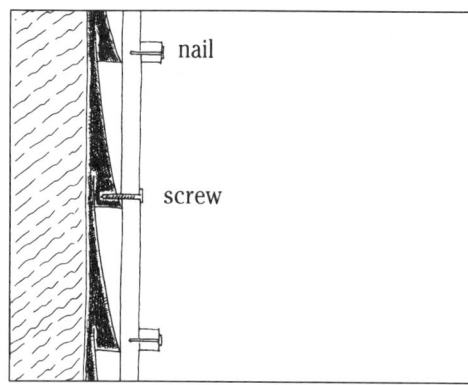

3. If the siding is narrow, you may have to skip every other panel for adequate spacing between horizontal strips.

This rose support can be modified for brick or masonry walls. To attach verticals, hold a vertical strip in place and drill through the strip into the wall, making certain the hole is deep enough to accommodate plastic mollies. Remove the strip, tap the mollies into place, reposition the strip, and attach with galvanized screws.

Suggested Plantings

Roses produce soft canes that require careful training upward in the early stages of growth. It's best to tie them into place with soft twine; wire cuts the canes. To encourage the plant to conform to your trellis, clip off any wayward canes as they appear.

Planting a bare–root rose is simple. Dig a large hole, then add a generous shovelful of sphagnum peat moss and a cup of bonemeal. Another good inexpensive fertilizer is dehydrated alfalfa in pellet form, available at feed stores. A scoop in each hole at planting time will produce amazing results. The alfalfa creates a chemical reaction in the soil, releasing important nutrients that are then absorbed by the rose. Although roses thrive on well-rotted manure, the odor of the alfalfa pellets is more pleasant—similar to a freshly mowed hay field.

Position the graft about 1 inch below the surface. If your building has a wide overhang, spread the root system out away from the wall toward the front of the bed to ensure that the plant will receive adequate moisture.

If potted roses are purchased, carefully lift the rose out of its container taking care not to disturb the ball of earth or potting mix. Prepare the hole as suggested for bare-root roses and refill it with soil about one inch above the graft. Gently tamp the earth around the rose to prevent air pockets from forming as you replace the soil around the root ball. Water both bare-root and container-grown roses every three or four days if the weather is dry until the plants become established.

Climbing roses are available for all regions of the country. My favorites include the following:

Coral pink: *Rosa* 'Aloha' has glossy, disease-resistant foliage and 3½-inch pink, double blooms. This hybrid pillar rose bears tea-shaped flowers with stems that are long enough for cutting.

Light pink: *Rosa* 'New Dawn', one of the most popular climbing roses of this century, produces masses of apple-blossom pink blooms from spring until frost. It is vigorous and disease-free.

Peach: Try *Rosa* 'Alchymist', which flowers profusely from spring to early summer. The dark green, glossy foliage of this vigorous plant is subtly colored with bronze tones that complement the orange-peach blossoms.

Deep red: *Rosa* 'Don Juan' is very fragrant and produces dark burgundy blooms with a velvet sheen. The plant grows 6 to 8 feet high, a manageable size for a trellis.

Yellow: *Rosa* 'Goldrush' lives up to its name and bears bright yellow, double flowers from spring through fall. The foliage is deep green, and the plant is extremely hardy. *R.* 'Yellow Rambler' is perfect for a trellis. Its bright, clear yellow double blooms appear primarily in the spring.

White: *Rosa* 'White Dawn' is related to the superb pink *R.* 'New Dawn', a sport—variation—of the old rambler 'Dr. Van Fleet'. Although it produces only half a dozen blossoms each season, its gardenia-shaped flowers are stunning. The foliage is a deep glossy green.

For *Southern or Southwestern gardeners*, I recommend *Rosa banksiae* 'Lutea', or Lady Banks Rose. This tender plant grows rapidly, exploding with tiny clusters of yellow, scented blooms on thornless canes. It demands space but deserves it. *R. banksiae alba plena* is the violet-scented form.

7
Wooden Free-Form Arched Trellis

WOODEN FREE-FORM ARCHED TRELLIS — 39

AN ARCHED FREE-FORM TRELLIS allows you to frame a special vine for dramatic vertical effect. At the same time, this garden feature helps enliven an uninteresting surface.

You can create an arched trellis by arranging vertical strips of varying lengths so that they form an arch. The number of strips you'll need depends on the size of the area you want to cover; the following instructions are for building a trellis 8 feet 9½ inches high by 10 feet 6 inches wide. If strips of 1x½–inch wood aren't available, have them ripped from 1x6–inch boards at a lumber mill.

Materials

Four strips of pressure-treated wood, 1x1½ inch by 10 feet 6 inches long
Seventeen strips of pressure-treated wood, 1x1 by 9 feet long
Plastic mollies
One box of size 5D nails
One box of galvanized 2-inch screws

Special Tools

Electric drill with masonry bit
Circular power saw
Tape rule
Safety glasses

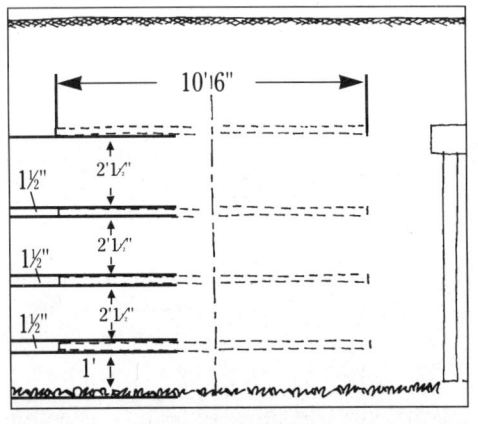

1. Using a tape rule, mark the location of the first horizontal strip 1 foot from ground level. Space the remaining three horizontal strips 2 feet 1½ inches apart, parallel to the first horizontal strip.

A brick wall supports a wooden free-form arched trellis covered with swags of dark green English ivy. It serves as an ideal foil for Rosa 'David Thompson', a hybrid rugosa rose, in the foreground. Design by Ezra Haggard.

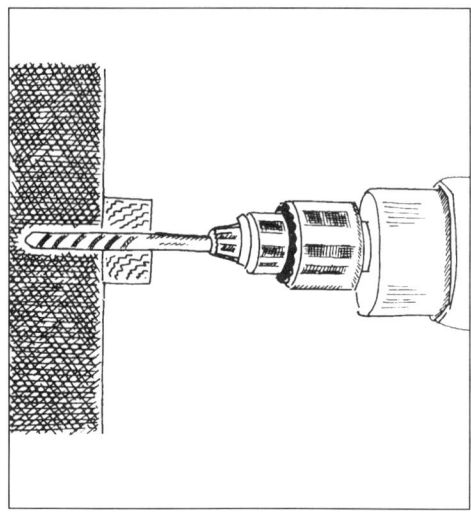

2. Attach each horizontal strip using four plastic mollies and 2-inch galvanized screws. Insert one screw 4 inches from each end, and space the remaining two equally. Hold one strip of wood in place and drill holes through the strip into the wall. Be sure your holes are deep enough to accommodate the anchors. Remove the strip, insert plastic mollies (anchors), reposition the strip, and screw into place.

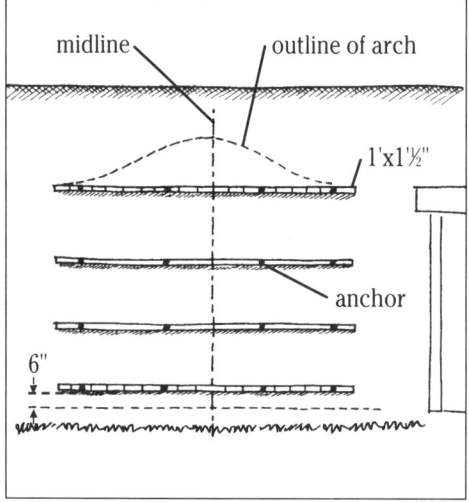

3. Mark the top and bottom horizontal strips at the midline. Make eight additional marks from these two points every 6 inches—to the right and to the left—for placement of vertical strips. Attach seventeen vertical strips, including the midline strip.

Suggested Plantings

Rosa rubrifolia (also called *R. glauca*) is a good choice for light shade and is hardy in most regions of the country. This species produces the most striking foliage of its genus—a soft, gray-green sprouting from mahogany-colored canes. The flowers are tiny (less than an inch wide), single, and a pale pink. The combination of *R. glauca* and the faded wood of a trellis against weathered red brick presents a striking picture.

Dutchman's-pipe *(Aristolochia durior)* is a rapid grower that thrives

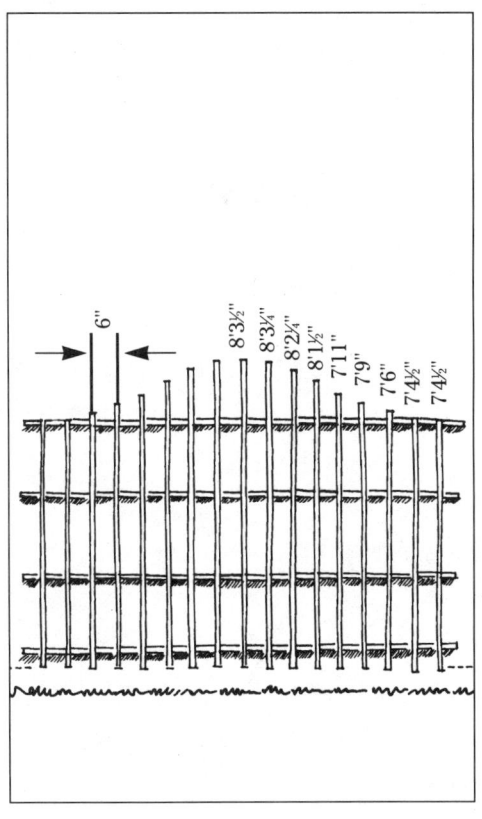

4. For the pattern shown, attach one midline vertical strip measuring 8 feet 3½ inches long. Cut the remaining sixteen vertical strips in pairs:

    8 feet 3¼ inches long
    8 feet 2¼ inches long
    8 feet 1½ inches long
    7 feet 11 inches long
    7 feet 9 inches long
    7 feet 6 inches long
    7 feet 4½ inches long (two pairs, a total of four)

Using the alignment marks on the horizontal strips, nail all vertical strips in pairs by length, beginning with the longest pairs, to the right and the left of the midline vertical. All vertical strips should hang 6 inches below the bottom horizontal strip.

in sun or shade and is covered with kidney-shaped leaves. The flowers are tubular and pipe-shaped with ivory-bronze coloring.

Climbing hydrangea *(Hydrangea anomala* subsp. *petiolaris)* is a woody vine with heart-shaped, evergreen leaves and stunning white clusters of spring flowers. Because its aerial rootlets cling to any surface, it is easy to train and prune.

If you want foliage with subtle coloring, plant *Actinidia kolomikta*. Its leaves are green with pink and white blotches at their tips, as if they had been painted. The flowers are tiny and sweetly scented.

Moonseed *(Menispermum canadense)* is a woody vine with heart-shaped foliage and small white flowers that bloom in spring. This twining vine is easily raised from seed and thrives in partial shade or filtered sunlight.

For fall bloom, try sweet autumn clematis *(Clematis paniculata)*. Your trellis will be smothered with frothy clusters of snowy flowers in late summer.

◆ 8 ◆

Wooden Enclosed Arched Trellis

WOODEN ENCLOSED ARCHED TRELLIS

THE BEAUTY OF a wooden enclosed arched trellis comes, in part, from its arched top. This design draws the eye upward while setting off both the vine and the perennials that surround its base. When attached to a brick chimney, it provides a dramatic backdrop for a bed of shrubs and flowers.

A wooden enclosed arched trellis is suitable against any wall—brick, stone, wood, or stucco. When selecting materials, be sure to purchase pressure-treated lumber.

Materials

One 2x4x½-inch sheet of plywood
One 4x8 sheet of prefabricated, small-hole lattice
Two ½x2-inch pieces of framing wood, 6 feet long
One ½x2-inch piece of framing wood, 3 feet 8 inches long
Four 6-foot pieces of 1x¼-inch lattice stripping
One box of size 4D nails
Eleven -inch lead anchors
Eleven lag bolts (¼ inch x 3 inches)

Special Tools

Electric drill with masonry bit (½-inch size)
Circular power saw
Jigsaw
Tape rule
Safety glasses

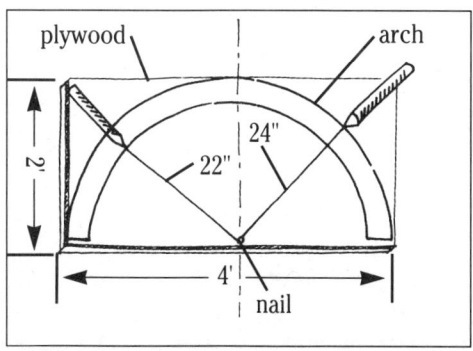

1. With string and pencil, draw an arch onto a 2x4x½-inch sheet of plywood.

A wooden arched trellis is a focal point, symmetrically anchored against a brick fireplace wall. Sprays of glossy, dark evergreen cotoneaster climb the trellis and create an airy effect above lemon balm and miscanthus grass. Design by Ezra Haggard.

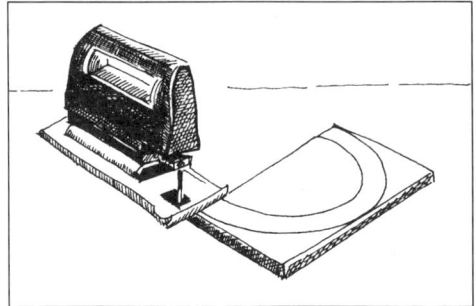

2. With string and pencil, draw an arch onto a 2x4x½-inch sheet of plywood.

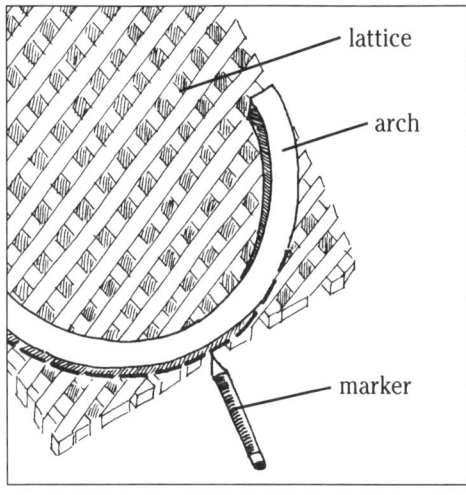

3. Place the plywood arch onto a 4x8 sheet of lattice and trace the outer circle.

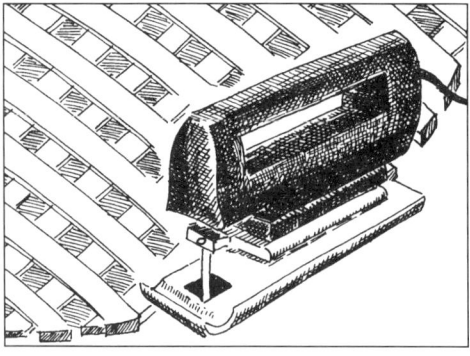

4. Cut the lattice arch with a jigsaw.

5. Assemble the wooden frame pieces for the trellis on a flat surface, such as a garage floor or driveway. Outer edges of framing pieces should be flush with outer edge of lattice. Nails should be placed 4 inches from the end of each framing piece (to prevent warping). Drive other nails, equally spaced approximately 1 foot apart, between nails at both ends. Nail the plywood arch onto the top curved portion of a 4x8 sheet of lattice Nail the side and bottom framing pieces to the trellis.

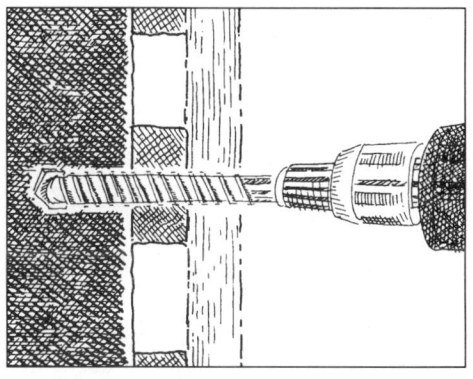

6. Hold the trellis against the wall, 6 inches from the ground, exactly where it will hang. Drill holes directly through the frame of the trellis into the wall. Use eleven anchoring points.

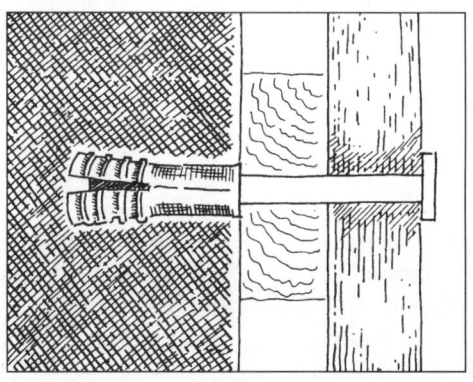

7. Remove the trellis and insert lead anchors. Mount the trellis with lag bolts.

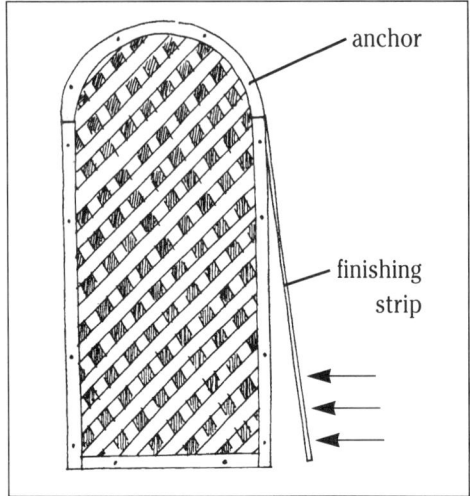

8. Add the outer lattice finishing strips, ¼x1 inch. These will bend to the shape of the trellis as you nail them intoplace.

Suggested Plantings

Consider the overall picture you want to create, including the trellis and the planting bed facing it. Keep in mind that the texture of the vine—its leaves and flowers—should complement the plants at its base.

Select your vines carefully; hardiness and growth habits vary depending on your climatic region. Decide whether you want annual vines such as morning–glory *(Ipomoea* spp.) or perennial vines (such as *Clematis* spp.), which continue to grow yearly but require careful pruning and shaping to stay within the bounds of your trellis.

Carefully prepare the soil at the base of the wall before planting your vine. Mix humus, leaf mold, or generous quantities of peat into the dug–out soil to make it richer, more friable; avoid adding fertilizers at this time. Try not to disturb the root ball as you set it in place. Water your vine thoroughly, then tie the stems to the trellis. Secure wandering growth and prune as necessary.

Northern gardeners might consider porcelain vine *(Ampelopsis brevipedunculata)*, which produces distinctive pale blue berries. Disease–free cultivars of honeysuckle are also a good choice; *Lonicera* 'Dropmore Scarlet' and *L.* 'Halliana' are both vigorous bloomers from spring until fall and tolerate light shade.

Southern gardeners can indulge in jasmine vines. The white confederate or star jasmine *(Trachelospermum jasminoides* 'Madison') is strongly scented and reliably hardy. It also tolerates light shade.

Pacific Northwest gardeners can choose *Ceanothus* X *delilianus* 'Gloire de Versailles', which is covered in mid-June with powder-blue clusters of flowers similar to those of lilacs. This plant is shrubby but can be trained to grow vertically.

For a hot, sunny location, try *Fremontodendron* 'California Glory'. It bears gray-green leaves and showers of bright yellow single flowers from spring until fall.

9

Wooden Cage and Tripod Rose Supports

WOODEN CAGE AND TRIPOD ROSE SUPPORTS

IF SPACE IN YOUR GARDEN is limited, consider building cage or tripod supports. These handy structures display vigorous roses at their best, adding height to the garden and allowing visitors to enjoy the blooms at a safe distance from the thorns. At the same time, they provide more room for the smaller hybrid teas, floribundas, and miniatures. By using these structures to support the large growers and planting other roses in the rest of the space, you can transform your bed into a impressive visual display.

Place wooden cage or tripod supports in the back or on the sides of the beds so that the shorter roses aren't competing for attention. You can build the supports around existing roses, or plant your roses first.

The following instructions are for building one cage rose support 4 feet high, 2 feet wide, and 2 feet deep. Be sure to use pressure-treated wood.

Materials

Four 2x2-inch posts, 5 feet long
Sixteen 1x2-inch cross pieces, 28 inches long
Four 1x2-inch top finishing strips, 24 inches long
One box of size 4D nails

Special Tools

Circular power saw
Miter box and saw
Builder's level
Tape rule

The canes of Rosa 'Baroness Rothschild' cascade over the top of a cage rose support. They are heavily laden with double pink, cupped blooms (forty petals each, with three blooms to a cluster.) Design by Ezra Haggard.

1. Tie up the rose.

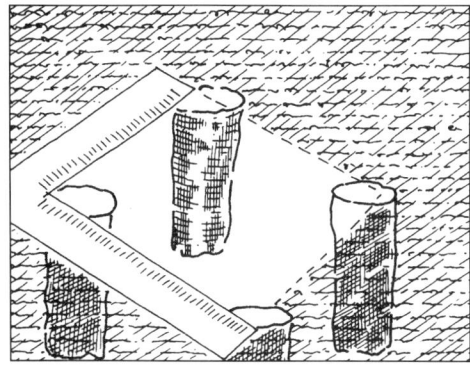

2. With a carpenter's steel square, mark the location of four holes 2 feet apart and dig the holes 1 foot deep.

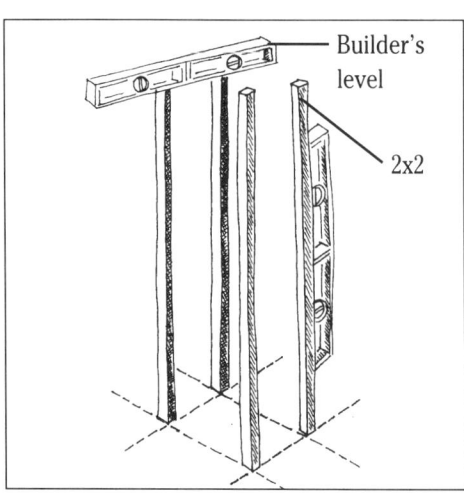

Builder's level

2x2

3. Insert the 5-foot-long 2x2s. Pack the holes loosely with soil. Using a builder's level, check the sides and tops of the verticals. Adjust as necessary so that the tops of the uprights are all the same height and vertical.

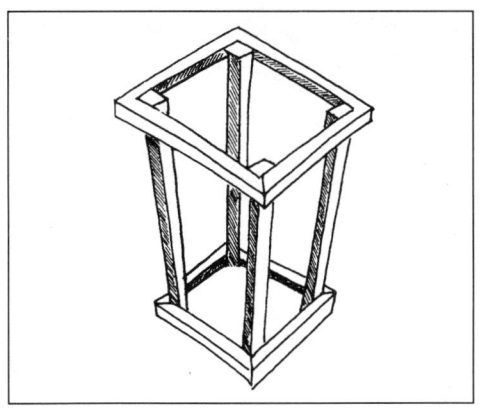

4. Miter and attach the cross pieces (1x2x28 inches) at ground level and at the top.

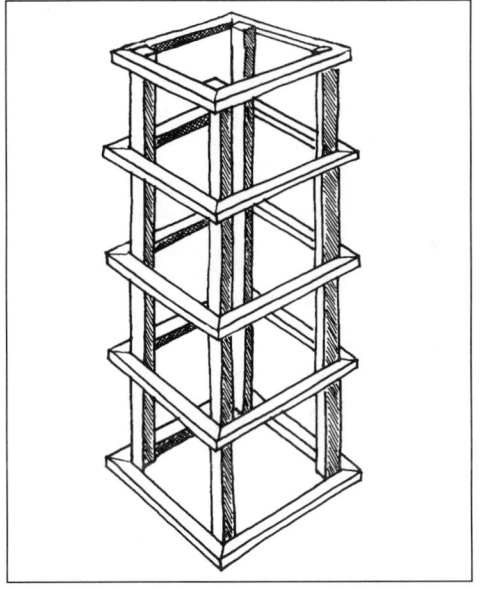

5. Attach three more sets of mitered cross pieces 1 foot apart.

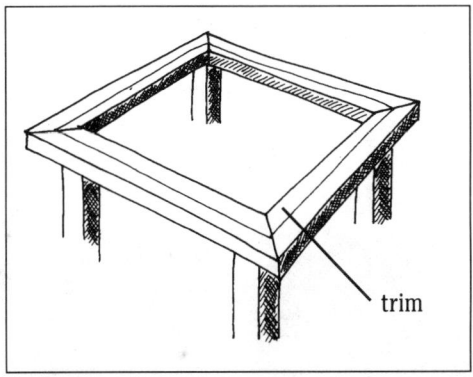

trim

6. Miter and nail the finishing strips (1x2x24 inches) into place at the top.

The following instructions are for building one tripod rose support 7 feet tall.

Materials

Three 8–foot–long 2x4s
One 12x12-inch board, ½ inch thick
One box of size 7D nails

Special Tools

Circular power saw
Tape rule

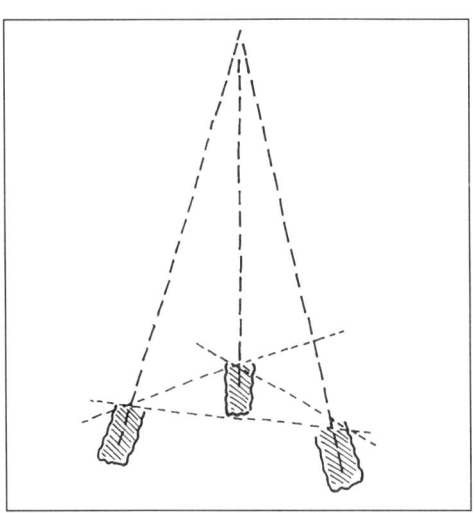

1. Tie up the existing rose, then dig three holes 1 foot deep, 2 ½ feet apart.

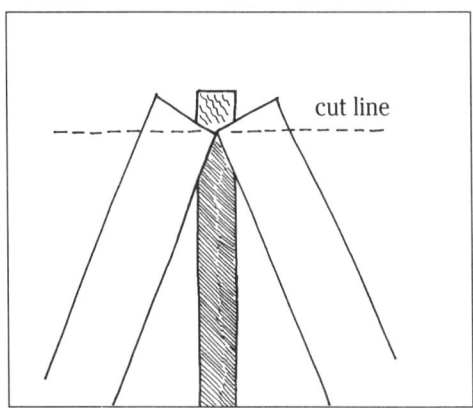

2. Place 2x4s into the holes, then align and mark the tops for cutting. Remove the 2x4s from the holes and saw off the tops so they are level.

WOODEN CAGE AND TRIPOD ROSE SUPPORTS

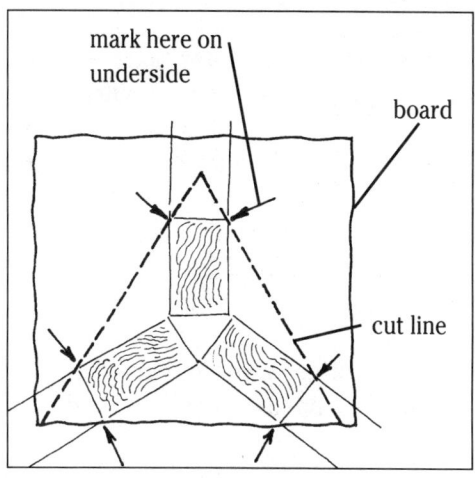

3. Lay the 6x6x½-inch board on top of the 2x4s. Mark the underside at points shown. Remove the cap, connect the marks with pencil lines, and saw into a triangle.

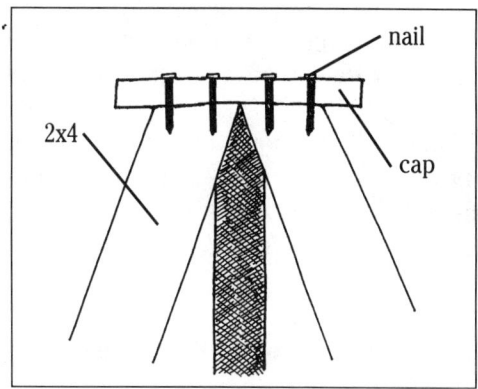

4. Nail the cap into place.

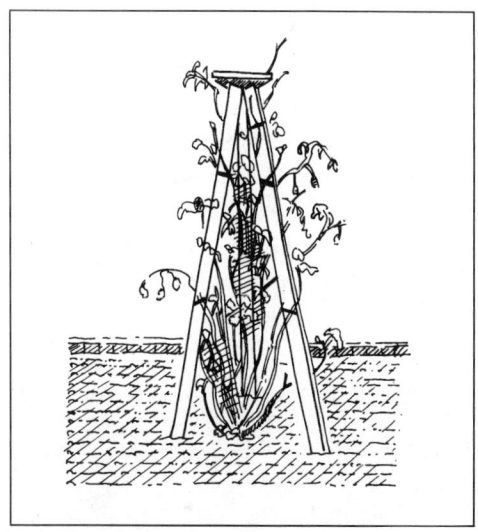

5. Untie the rose. Clip, tie, and shape the long canes to conform to the tripod support.

Suggested Plantings

For suggested roses and their cultivation, see Chapter Six. Climbers, ramblers, species roses, and many antique shrub roses are suitable for growing in cage or tripod supports. When planting vigorous, tall-growing roses, add a few extra spadesful of alfalfa pellets or well-rotted manure to help get them started.

Additional roses for *continual bloom* include the following:

White: *Rosa* 'Aimée Vibert' and *R.* 'Mme. Alfred Carrière' produce large double blooms in clusters that usually repeat bloom during the summer and fall.

Red: *Rosa* 'Climbing Crimson Glory' offers double, very fragrant, deep purple-red blooms. It is dependably hardy anywhere, and suitable for cutting.

Pink: *Rosa* 'America' has spicy, hybrid-tea-shaped flowers with dark, leathery foliage. It is dependably hardy and disease-resistant.

Yellow: *Rosa* 'Golden Showers' bears bright narcissus–yellow flowers with a light scent. The dark, glossy foliage covers vigorous canes that are almost thornless.

Apricot-peach: *Rosa* 'Royal Sunset' has blooms measuring over 4 inches wide and shaped like a hybrid tea. The foliage is a striking coppery-green and very disease-resistant.

For those who prefer antique roses and *one–time bloomers*, I suggest the following:

White: *Rosa* 'Félicité et Perpétue' (1827), a vigorous old-time favorite, has tiny pom–pom like blooms with a scent reminiscent of green apples.

Pink: *Rosa* 'May Queen' (1898) bears lush, clear lilac-pink flowers that are very fragrant. The foliage is disease-resistant. A modern one-time bloomer is *Rosa* 'Constance Spry' (1961). Its old-fashioned blooms are cabbage–shaped and have a powerful myrrh-like scent.

Red: *Rosa* 'Parkdirector Riggers' (1957) is a vigorous grower that will tolerate some shade. Its clear, bright red flowers appear in large clusters in summer and, if you're lucky, may bloom more than once.

Apricot-orange: *Rosa* 'Leontyne Gervais' (1903) is a rambler with dense, glossy foliage and wide, fragrant, apricot–orange-colored blooms. It is reliably hardy and a vigorous grower.

Ready-Mix Concrete Projects

10

Free-Form Flagstones

Free-form flagstones placed in a shady woodland garden are surrounded by sweet woodruff (Galium odoratum) *and a white cranesbill.* Design by Tim Morehouse.

Do you have a flat, bare area on your property where grass burns out early in the summer and perennial ground covers, such as ivy, pachysandra, or vinca, require weeding? Are nearby tree roots robbing the surface soil of nutrients and moisture? If so, consider constructing a stone terrace and growing special plants among the stones. As the eminent English gardener V. Sackville-West once observed, " Many plants do better if they can get their roots under stones... The reason, obviously, is that they never suffer from excessive moisture or excessive drought." *(V. Sackville-West's Garden Book,* ed. Philippa Nicolson, Atheneum, New York, 1983.)

If natural fieldstones or flagstones aren't available or are too expensive, you can construct your own "stones" right on the spot. Choose a site for your free–form flagstones that is at least 12 feet by 12 feet. Grade the surface until it is smooth, then rake it flat. If large tree roots are in the way, you may have to remove them or simply work around them.

If you want to draw attention to a specimen plant in the center of your terrace, plant it first in good soil, then stand back and see how it looks in relation to the whole picture. For other plants, select areas where they will go between the stones. Make sure there are areas where visitors can walk or stand without harming the plants.

Materials

One 75–pound bag of ready-mix concrete for two stones (thirty bags may be necessary for a 12x12–foot patio, depending on the size of your stones)
Brown concrete dye (optional; approximately 1 cup per bag of concrete)
Builder's sand
One 25-foot roll of chicken wire
Enough burlap to cover the area

Special Tools

Stiff wire brush
Wire cutters

FREE-FORM FLAGSTONES

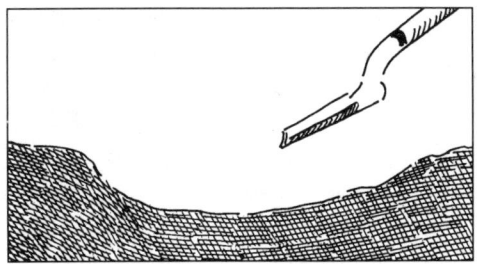

1. With a spade, scoop out holes about 4 to 5 inches deep. Shape these holes to look like natural flagstones, varying the size as you prepare the spaces. Stand back and view the results as you dig and shape.

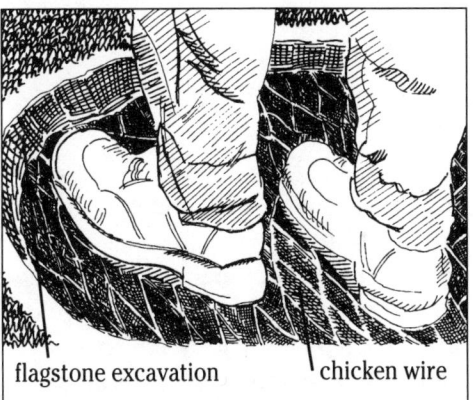

flagstone excavation   chicken wire

2. For added support as the concrete hardens, line each hole with chicken wire. Make certain the wire is well below the surface. If necessary, tamp it down with your feet.

3. Follow the directions on the bags of mortar mix. If you want your stones to look even more like natural sandstone, add a brown concrete dye while preparing the mixture. Fill one hole at a time with the mixture to cover the chicken wire. Shape the surface of each stone with a trowel; aim for a natural look.

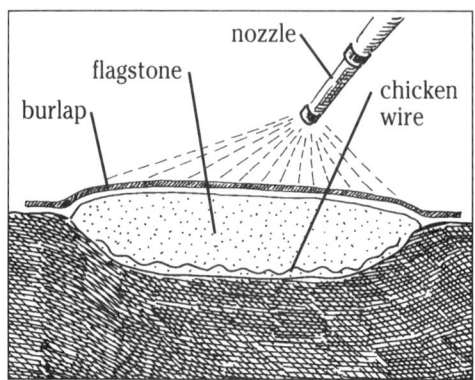

4. Cover the entire area with damp burlap, and spray lightly with a hose (use the fine-mist setting). The next day, rub the surface of each stone with a stiff wire brush to produce a more natural texture. For the next three or four days, spray the area lightly to prevent the concrete from hardening too quickly.

Suggested Plantings

Once your flagstones are dry, you can install the plants. If your soil is a heavy clay, replace it with equal proportions of pea gravel, sand, and good friable topsoil.

Consider the light requirements of your selections. For example, if your terrace is located in a woodland setting surrounded by large oak trees, try planting acid-loving shrubs such as azaleas along the border. Be sure to incorporate generous quantities of sphagnum peat moss.

Hostas may be useful as underplantings among smaller shrubs. *Hosta* 'Kabitan' is a good choice; it is low-growing and has lance-shaped, yellow-green leaves. The smaller blue hostas such as *H.* 'Hadspun Heron', *H.* 'Hadspun Blue', and *H.* 'Blue Wedgewood' are also suitable.

Between your free-form stones, try creepers such as *Ajuga* 'Burgundy Glow', *A.* 'Metallica crispa', *Sedum ternatum,* and European ginger *(Asarum europaeum).* The tiny spring bulbs—crocus, grape hyacinths, miniature daffodils, and snowdrops—mingle well with the creepers. Cranesbills *(Geranium* 'Johnson's Blue', 'Ballerina', and 'Lancastriense') bloom in late spring and occasionally during the summer. Sweet woodruff *(Galium odoratum)* will provide a fine, delicate texture between the stones but it spreads quickly.

Grow what appeals to you, but be aware of the scale of your terrace; plants will increase with each passing year and seed themselves at random. Your design doesn't have to be static, however. If a plant doesn't satisfy you, rip it out and replace it with one that does.

11

Miniature Reflecting Pools

POOLS OF WATER in rocks or stones are an arresting feature in a landscape. Imagine a small pool in a secluded wooded area, a rock garden, a corner of the terrace, or a flower border—the possibilities are endless. Unfortunately, natural rock or stone formations that hold water can be difficult to find, and installing them can involve great expense and labor. Volcanic stones, though lightweight, are costly and often

A miniature reflecting pool placed on an ivy-covered stump in a woodland garden makes a naturalistic birdbath. Design by Tim Morehouse.

look unnatural if placed at random on flat ground among shrubs and perennials.

There is a relatively inexpensive and easy way to add a natural touch of water to your garden by building a miniature reflecting pool. With little effort, you can create a tiny body of water that will attract birds and catch the reflection of clouds and blue sky overhead. A miniature reflecting pool is an ornament—one you can create quickly from your own molds or simply by shaping a pile of stiff mortar mix into an artificial stone. These tiny pools blend naturally with any garden setting and, if they are portable, can be moved as easily as you would a birdbath.

The instructions that follow are for building two shapes: a circle 12 inches in diameter and light enough to move around the garden, and a larger pool measuring 2 feet in diameter (roughly the size of a millstone), which remains where you pour and shape the mortar mix.

Materials

One bag of ready-mix concrete (makes three small pools, each 12 inches in diameter and 6 inches deep, or one large millstone–shaped pool, roughly 2 feet wide and 8 inches high); the sand-cement blend is easiest to handle

One kitchen bowl (mixing bowl, salad bowl, etc.) 12 inches in diameter and 6 inches deep

A smaller bowl approximately 4 inches wide and 4 inches deep

Plastic trash can liners or garment bags to line the bowls

Builder's sand

Peat moss

Tiny stones about 1 inch in diameter for decorating the rim of a circular reflecting pool (optional)

Special Tools

Trowel

Stiff wire brush

Portable Reflecting Pool

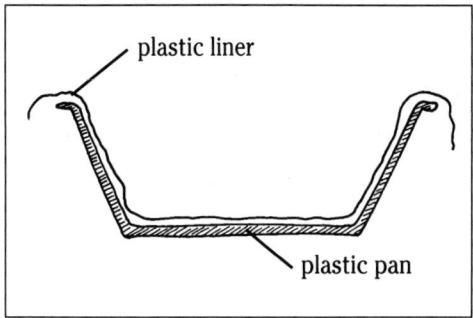

1. Mix the mortar according to the directions on the bag. Keep some extra dry mixture handy in case your ingredients become too watery. Make a stiff mixture, but be sure all of the particles are moistened. Line the large bowl with a sheet of plastic.

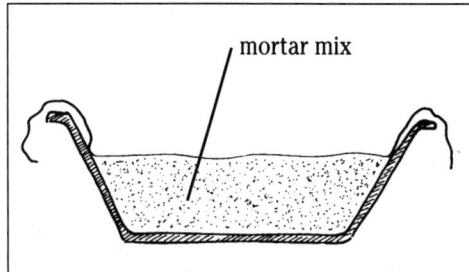

2. Fill the container with the cement mixture. Flatten or smooth the top with a trowel.

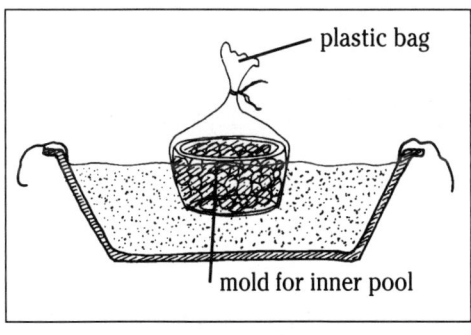

3. Cover the outside of the smaller bowl with plastic and plunge it into the center of the larger bowl. Place a weight on top (a large stone or brick) or use smaller stones within the bowl to keep it submerged.

4. Use a trowel to smooth the rim.

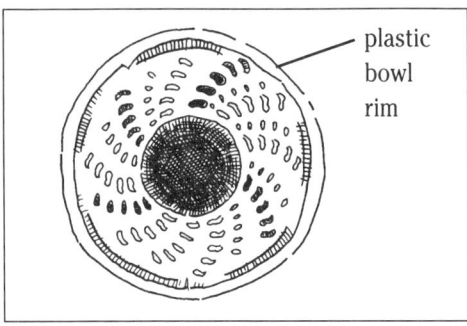

plastic bowl rim

5. If you like, add small stones around the outside rim of the larger bowl before the mixture dries.

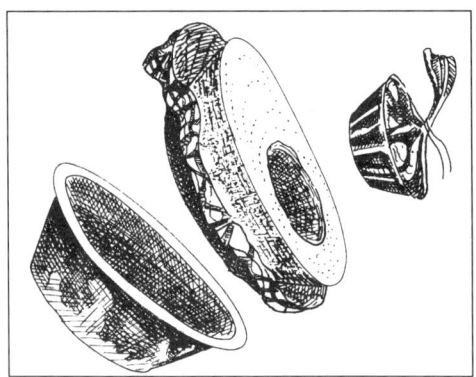

6. After the molds dry, remove the smaller bowl first, then the larger bowl. Both bowls should slip away easily because of the plastic liners. You'll notice wrinkled marks formed by the plastic as you strip it off; these will eventually be filled in with moss and will add to the overall design.

7. To give a natural finish to your miniature pool, sprinkle builder's sand and peat over the inside and outside surfaces, then rub them with a stiff wire brush.

MINIATURE REFLECTING POOLS _____ 65

A round concrete pool (only 6 inches wide and 6 inches deep) is placed in the border to catch the reflections of blue forget-me-nots mingling with the lacy fronds of English crested ferns. Design by Tim Morehouse.

In Situ Reflecting Pool

1. Thoroughly mix the concrete, adding only enough water to make a stiff mixture. Using your trowel, shape the pile of cement into a natural-looking stone measuring approximately 2 feet wide and 8 inches high.

2. Line the outside of a small kitchen bowl with plastic and sink it into the deeper end of your "stone" to form the pool. Weigh it down with a stone or brick. Twenty-four hours later, remove the bowl and plastic liner. Sprinkle builder's sand and peat moss over the surface and rub it with a stiff wire brush.

Suggested Plantings

Place your artificial stone or miniature pool where it can attract birds—for example, near a clump of azaleas and hart's-tongue ferns *(Asplenium scolopendrium)* or maidenhair ferns *(Adiantum pedatum)*. Rock garden plants, such as tiny spring bulbs or primulas, are also suitable for planting near reflecting pools.

12

Trough Gardens

*A trough garden containing leafy stonecrop (*Sedum dasyphyllum*) and a soft pink cranesbill (*Geranium sanguineum var. striatum*). Design by Tim Morehouse.*

BRITISH GARDENERS HAVE a wonderful knack for tucking tiny alpines and other small treasures into antique troughs or sinks once used by farmers for watering hogs and cattle. Today, these troughs are almost impossible to find, and their cost is prohibitive. But you can still create a miniature trough garden by building your own concrete container.

To begin your project, you'll need to build a plywood mold—both an outer and inner box—to keep the trough from buckling before the concrete cures. Remember that two people will need to lift the trough onto support blocks when it is ready for planting, so keep the dimensions manageable. A good overall size for the exterior mold is 18 inches long, 12 inches wide, and 12 inches deep; the inner mold, which forms the walls of your trough as well as the planting area, should be 13 inches long and 7 inches wide.

The following instructions are for building one trough 18 inches by 12 inches by 12 inches.

Materials

One bag of ready-mix concrete (the sand–cement mixture is best)
One 4x8 sheet of plywood, cut into appropriate lengths and widths for constructing the inner box (13x7x12) and the outer box (18x12x12)
One box of size 4D nails
Plastic trash or garment bags for lining both boxes
Two 2-inch corks or tiny flowerpots for drainage holes
Rabbit-hutch wire

Special Tools

Jigsaw
Wire cutters
Stiff wire brush

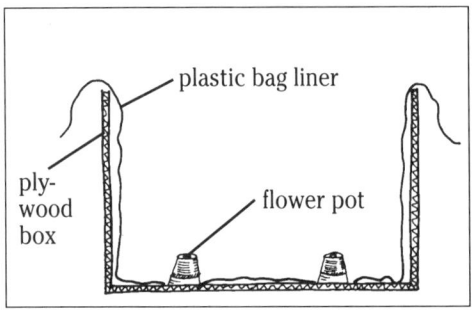

1. Cut out the plywood for the sides and bottoms of both boxes, and build the molds. Line the inside of the exterior box with plastic. After lining the box, place several corks or tiny flowerpots on top of the plastic covering the bottom.

TROUGH GARDENS 69

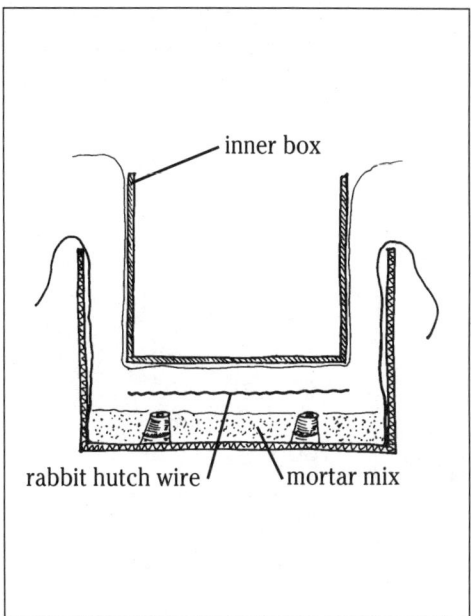

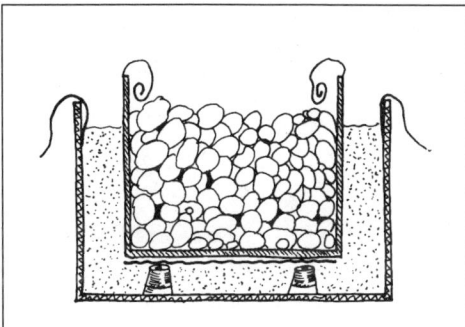

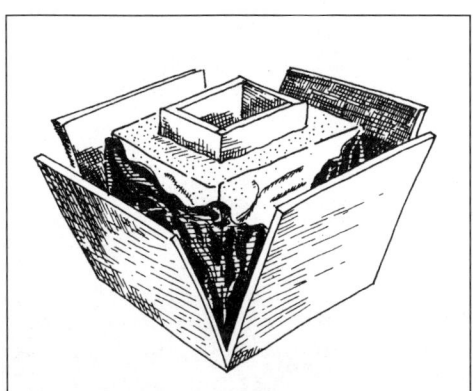

2. Pour into the bottom of the exterior mold about 2 inches of mortar—approximately the depth of the corks or flowerpots, which will serve as drainage holes. Cut a piece of wire mesh 13 inches long x 7 inches wide, and place it over the drainage area, on top of the corks or flowerpots. (It will be secured by the mortar mixture.) Wrap the exterior of the second box with plastic and immediately center it on top of the wet mortar. The space between the outer and inner boxes will be approximately 2 inches.

3. Place a few bricks or stones inside the second container to secure its position. Pour mortar mix between the two boxes to form the four sides. Using a trowel, stir the mixture to break up air pockets. Allow the molds to dry for 24 hours or until the mixture has set.

4. Carefully remove the outside mold by pulling away the four sides as shown. Turn the trough on its side and remove the bottom of the form, then strip away the plastic lining.

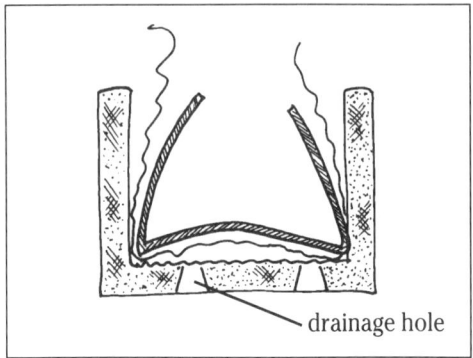

drainage hole

5. Remove the sides and bottom of the inside mold.

6. Dig out the corks or flowerpots with an old screwdriver to clear the drainage holes.

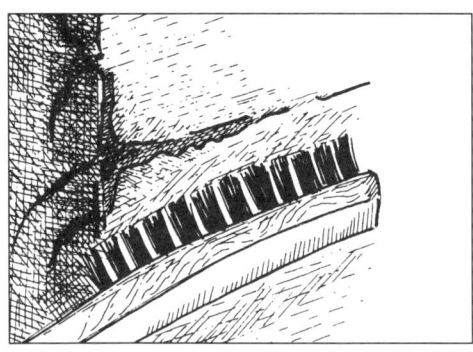

7. Use a stiff wire brush to scrape away the pieces of plastic and give a weathered, antique look to your trough. Eventually, moss will fill in the rough surfaces and enhance the natural appearance of the container.

TROUGH GARDENS

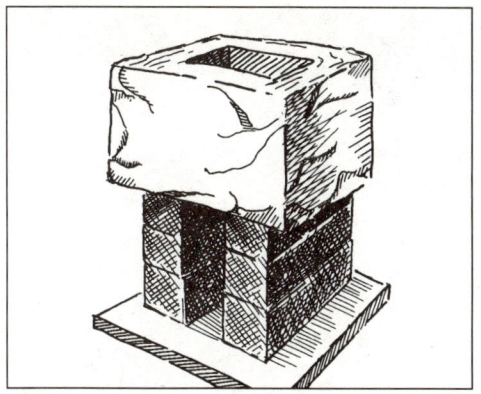

8. Display the trough on bricks stacked to form two pedestals or on concrete blocks placed on a hard, flat surface. Fill the bottom with a 2-inch layer of crushed stones, then add soil mixture and plants.

Suggested Plantings

Russell Page, in his classic work *The Education of a Gardener*, wrote, "Remember that one of your aims must be to lift people, if only for a moment, above their daily preoccupations... a glimpse of beauty outside will enable them to make a healing contact with their own inner world." Designing and planting trough gardens is one way to do this. Homemade concrete troughs are perfect for displaying compact flowering gems that would otherwise be lost in the garden. Positioned beside or within a long border or on the sunny side of a patio, these containers create a miniature landscape, a living entity that can provide subtle beauty throughout the seasons.

The soil mixture for your trough garden should consist of four parts loam, one part sphagnum peat, one part leaf compost, two parts coarse sand, and four parts grit or stone chips. This mixture can be adjusted easily to suit the demands of the plants you choose. For example, you can substitute limestone chips for lime-loving plants or increase the amount of peat for acid-loving plants. Check with your local nursery or garden center for plants' soil requirements.

Gardeners living in any zone, from the Pacific Northwest to New England, can enjoy a variety of dwarf and miniature plants in their trough gardens.

Northwestern gardeners can focus on the more exotic alpines. The scree conditions of this region will support rock jasmine (*Androsace* spp.), heather (*Erica* spp.), gentiana, lewisias, pinks (*Dianthus* spp.), and saxifrages (especially the Kabschia varieties). Persian candytuft (*Aethionema* 'Wendy Rose'), a slow-growing shrublet only 6 inches high, is another good choice for the Pacific Northwest. In May, every

*A trough overflowing with mother-of-thyme (*Thymus serpyllum*) and cranesbill (*Geranium sanguineum* var. striatum) creates a miniature landscape within the garden.* Design by Tim Morehouse.

tiny twig bursts into bloom with bright pink flowers that are identical in shape to those of the popular *Daphne cneorum*.

Midwestern gardeners could plant veronicas, moss campion (*Silene acaulis*), thrift (*Armeria* spp.), saxifrages, sedums, and sempervivums. *Erodium chamaedryoides* 'Roseum' produces tiny pink flowers similar to those of cranesbill and is effective in trough gardens, as is mother-of-thyme (*Thymus serpyllum*). Four–inch–tall *Potentilla verna* 'Nana' has yellow blooms that appear in May; *Primula modesta* is another spring gem for a trough.

Southwestern gardeners might choose among the echeverias in shades of pink, lavender, and silver-blue. One particularly striking species is *Echeveria peacockii*, which has succulent, pale blue leaves with a pink blush. Don't despair if you live in Zone 5 or 6: you can still use these beautiful plants as long as you keep them in a cool greenhouse or on a basement window ledge during the winter months.

Northeastern gardeners can select *Allium cyaneum, Alyssum condensatum,* rock jasmine (*Androsace* spp.), rock cress (*Arabis* spp.), *Aubrieta deltoidea* (which forms trailing mats of blue, red, pink, and purple flowers), sedums, and sempervivums.

Gardeners in Zones 3 to 5 who must endure several bleak months of cold weather might plant a trough entirely with cobweb houseleek *(Sempervivum arachnoideum)* and a fastigiate juniper such as *Juniperis communis* var. 'Compressa'. The gray-green combination creates a delightful winter scene.

Other suitable dwarf conifers include *Chamaecyparis obtusa* 'Nana', *C. obtusa* 'Snowkist', *C. obtusa* 'Spiralis', *Picea abies* 'Little Gem', and *Tsuga canadensis* 'Pygmaea' (a three-year-old specimen may stand only 3 inches high). Keep in mind that some of these miniatures prefer shade during the hottest part of the day if the air is dry. Junipers and pines are sun-lovers.

Seek cultural advice from a reliable nurseryman, and select plants whose roots prefer the cool cover of stone and sharp drainage. Look for plants that sprawl and provide color. Or consider green trailing plants that bloom for only a short period but add visual interest throughout the growing season, such as thyme or *Aurinia* and its cultivars: *Aurinia saxatilis* 'Silver Queen', a pale yellow; 'Rosie O'Day', a deep rose; and 'Royal Carpet', violet.

A trough allows you to experiment on a small scale. If a plant doesn't fit, take it out. Your arrangements aren't static; learn to add and subtract, and don't be afraid to be ruthless.

Pools and Fountains

13

Informal Pool

An informal pool surrounded by natural fieldstones and a single jet of water to provide sound add a dimension of tranquility to the garden. Design by Ezra Haggard.

THE IDEA of an informal pool in the landscape is tempting to most gardeners. Pool supply departments in nursery centers fuel the imagination, but you must resist the urge to go overboard. Envision your site as a whole composition, and think of a pool of water—beautiful and exciting though it may be—as only part of your landscape.

Consider the shape of your pool before you begin. Kidney or oval shapes are often considered to be the most natural, but if placed in the middle of a lawn, they can look hackneyed.

Choose your site carefully; the water should blend well with your planting schemes. Keep in mind that visitors don't want to see all the features of your garden at once.

The location of your informal pool is important for practical reasons, too. For example, it's best to avoid placing a pool below trees; decomposing leaves will kill fish, and the shade will thwart any attempts to grow water lilies.

When selecting a site, keep in mind that water lilies require warm temperatures and at least half a day of sunlight and will do even better in full sun. Wind is also a factor; a still surface is best if you want water lilies to bloom. Remember, too, that a sheltered site will warm up more quickly in the sun, and if you add a waterfall, it won't be disturbed by sudden gusts of wind.

A depression or low-lying area on your property may seem an ideal location for a pool, but heavy rainfall can cause erosion, and muddy water is not appealing. If you decide such an area is still the best (or only) site, you can elevate the pool, build up stones around it, and fill the adjacent hollow with bog plants.

As you dig the area, you can mound the excavated soil up behind the pool to make a series of slopes, then add partially embedded stones in this bank of soil and plants that will reflect in the water's surface. One or two mounds, layered with stones of varying sizes, would also make a good spot for a waterfall. Build the soil and rocks up gradually, and keep the mounds low; steep slopes behind or along the sides of the pool can erode, causing soil to wash into the water.

Edge your informal pool with stones that are indigenous to your area. Fieldstones are flat, round, or irregularly shaped; flagstones are quarried and commonly used for stepping–stones. Both work well as edging. Place your stones so that they hang over the edge several inches. Be sure to set the stones in place carefully and securely so that the liner doesn't show. Careful arrangement of edging stones also prevents rainwater from draining into the pool.

If you like, you can dig a shelf around all or part of your pool for con-

INFORMAL POOL _____ 79

tainerized water plants. You can also use parts of this shelf to hold partially submerged boulders, which will enhance the natural look of the pond.

If you plan to use a pump to recirculate the pool water, add a fountain or cascading water, or put in underwater lights, hire a licensed electrician before installing such equipment. A professional can advise you on safety as well as any city codes that may apply regarding outside electrical fixtures in your area. A word of caution: small children are always attracted to water.

The following instructions are for constructing a pool 7 feet wide by 10 feet long by 18 inches deep.

Materials

Butyl or PVC (polyvinylchloride) liner. To determine the size of the liner needed, add twice the depth of the pool to its width and to its length. If pool is 8 feet wide x 10 feet long x 2 feet deep, you will need 8 feet plus 4 feet (2 x 2-foot depth), which equals 12 feet. This is the width of the liner. Ten feet plus 4 feet (2 x 2-foot depth) equals 14 feet. This is the length of the liner. Buy a liner 12 x 14 feet or the next larger size if this is not available.

Builder's sand

Stones for edging

Pump for recycling water (optional)

Special Tools

Builder's level

2x4 approximately 8 feet long (or the width of your pool)

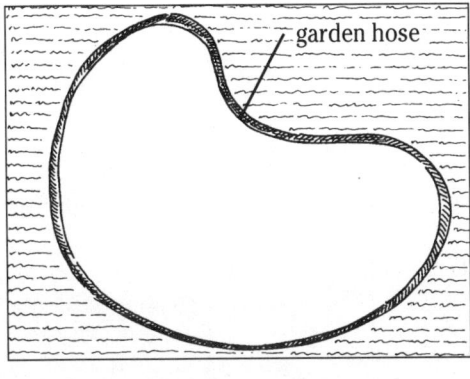

1. Choose a flat surface and arrange a rubber garden hose in the shape you want.

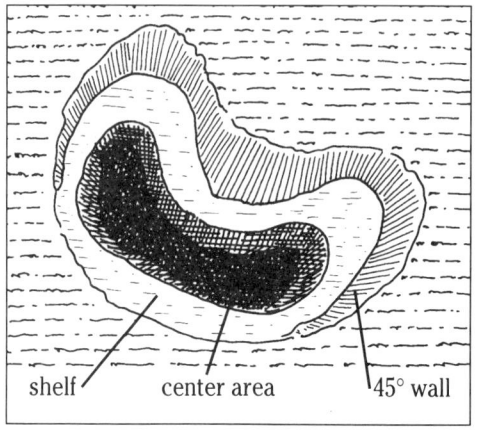

2. Dig out the shelf first (optional); it should measure 9 inches wide and sit 9 inches below the water rim. Next, dig out an additional 9 inches to form the base. Dig at a 45–degree angle so that the sides slope inward. Remove any large stones or roots, since they can puncture the liner.

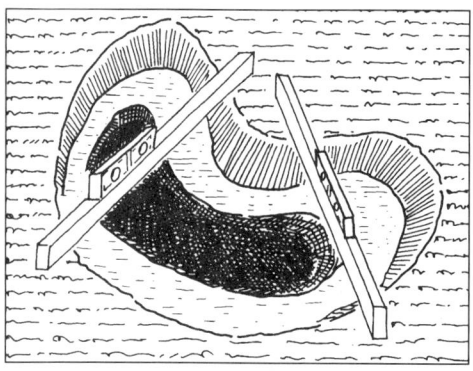

3. Check the ledge of the pool to make sure it is level. Use a straight piece of 2x4 and a builder's level across the edges. Remove excess soil, if necessary, until the ledge is precisely level all around the pool.

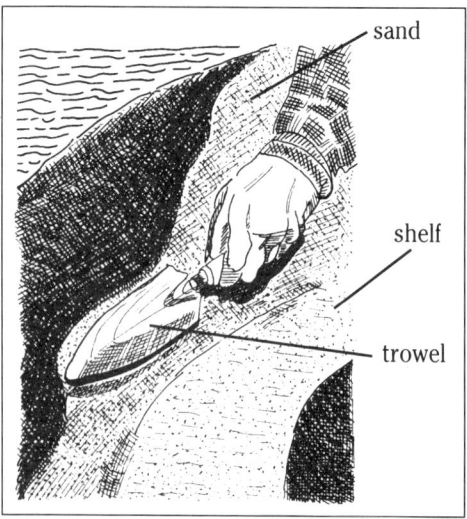

4. Cover the sides and bottom of the pool with moistened sand.

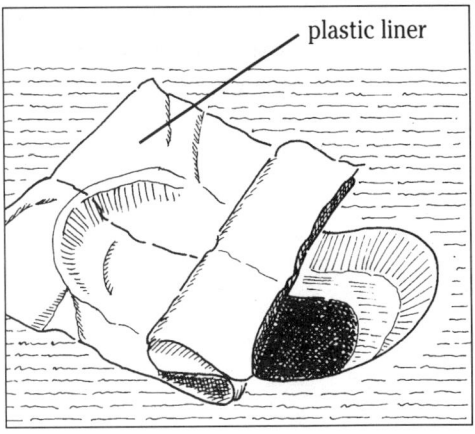

5. Place a folded PVC or Butyl liner in the middle of the pool and unfold it into position. Install the liner on a warm, sunny day so that it will be more pliable.

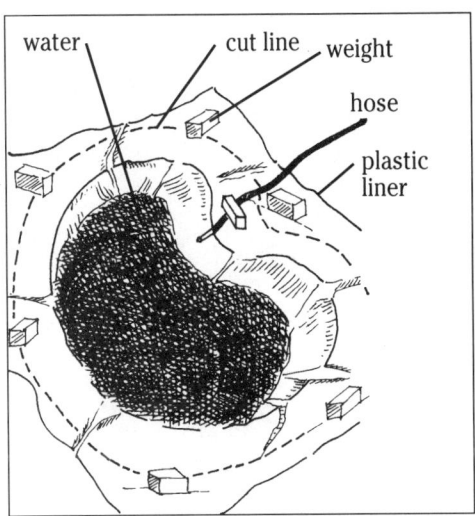

6. Place a hose in the center of the liner and fill slowly with water, stretching the sides gently and working out large creases as the pool fills. Place stones or bricks around the edge of the liner to stabilize it while filling.

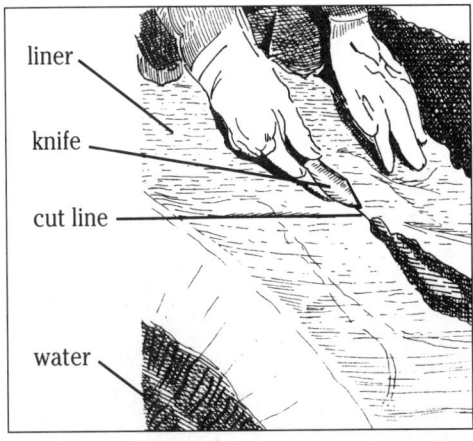

7. When the water is 2 inches from the rim, trim back the excess portion of the liner with scissors or a sharp knife. The edging strip should be about 8 inches wide.

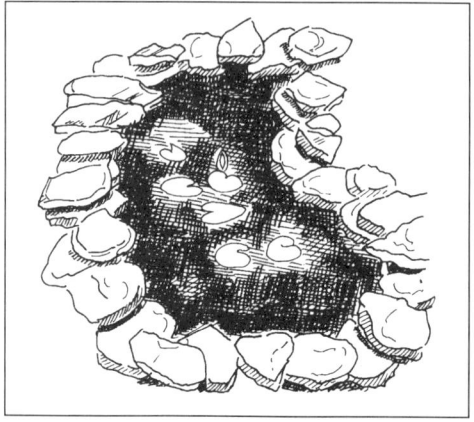

8. Lay flat stones around the edge to conceal the exposed portion of the liner.

Suggested Plantings

A hardy bog or shallow water plant that will flourish in all zones is arrowhead (*Sagittaria* spp.), which produces white spikes of flowers and leaves that are shaped as its name suggests. There are both single (*S. latifolia*) and double (*S.* 'Florepleno') forms available.

The hardy calla *(Calla palustris)* bears heart-shaped leaves the first year and small white calla-like flowers the second. It does best in the moist soil found near the water's edge.

For a boggy area near the pool, plant cardinal flower *(Lobelia cardinalis)*. Its stately spikes of fiery red flowers, similar to those of delphinium, would make an attractive reflection in the water.

Blue iris *(Iris versicolor)* is the perfect partner for yellow iris *(I. pseudacorus)*. Both grow to a height of 2 to 3 feet in wet or boggy soil and bear broad, sword-shaped leaves.

Dwarf sweet flag *(Acorus gramineus)* is a slender, smaller version of common sweet flag *(A. calamus)* and is ideal near the pool's edge. It produces 8- to 10-inch grassy tufts of foliage that give off a spicy citrus scent when bruised.

The beautiful marsh marigold *(Caltha palustris)* is one of the earliest water plants to flower in spring. It produces a profusion of rich gold blooms that resemble buttercups.

An informal pool would not be complete without cattails. The dwarf species *(Typha minima)* grows 1 to 1½ feet tall and produces light brown, egg-shaped catkins. This is a tender species and must be moved indoors for the winter.

Pickerel rush *(Pontederia cordata)* is effective placed 4 or 5 inches below the pool's surface or near the edge. This fine blue-flowered plant grows about 2 feet tall and has smooth, shiny olive-green leaves.

Southern, Southwestern, or Pacific Coast gardeners can enjoy tropical water plants, including purple water hyacinth *(Eichhornia azurea)*, a creeping plant without floating bulbs, but with more showy flowers than those of the common water hyacinth.

Water poppy *(Hydrocleys nymphoides)* produces deep green, floating leaves and bright yellow, three-petaled flowers.

Sword plants *(Echinodorus* spp.*)* are tall leafy plants that grow to over 3 feet in height and change color with the seasons: the young foliage is bright red, and the color fades to olive, then dark green. White flowers bloom high above the water's surface.

For a delightful little plant, try water snowflake *(Nymphoides indica)*, which bears small, heart-shaped leaves that float on the surface. Its delicate white flowers have yellow centers.

Dwarf papyrus *(Cyperus haspan* var. *viviparus)* is an attractive aquatic foliage plant with threadlike leaves and round mop heads. This is a dwarf form of Egyptian paper plant *(Cyperus papyrus)*.

A water plant that is content to grow in or out of the water is the popular umbrella plant *(Cyperus alternifolius)*. Grassy umbrellalike heads of leaves stand 3 to 5 feet tall.

Gardeners living in areas where winters are severe can also grow tropical water plants, but they must bring these plants indoors. Use basket-weave containers for planting submerged species so that you can rearrange them easily and control vigorous spreading. Check with a good nursery supplier for advice on pond containers and their use.

There are two kinds of water lilies *(Nymphaea* spp.*)*: the hardy species, including *Nymphaea odorata* and *N. tuberosa*, and the tropical species. The hardy will thrive anywhere outdoors, but the tropical must be lifted or treated as annuals and wintered over in a greenhouse, warm garage, or basement if you live in a cold zone. Southern, Southwestern, and Pacific Coast gardeners can indulge in either kind if they live where temperatures do not drop below 40 degrees F. for extended periods of time. A garden center specializing in pond supplies (or a mail–order source) can tell you which water lilies flourish in your region.

If you're thinking about growing water lilies in your pool, keep in mind some of the major differences between the hardy and tropical kinds:

Tropical
1) Strongly aromatic
2) Many blooms per plant

3) Flower buds held above the water's surface
4) All colors
5) Many night-blooming varieties

Hardy
1) Slight or no aroma
2) Single to many blooms
3) Flowers float on surface of pool
4) No blue or purple shades
5) No night bloomers

To maintain the natural look of your informal pool, don't destroy the illusion with fancy fountains splashing in the center or with water that's too clear; a dark green depth will add a certain mystery to the pool. On the other hand, the water should be clear enough that you can see the fish darting about—that is, environmentally balanced. Bacteria in your pool will convert organic wastes (produced by the fish) to nontoxic nutrients (used by the water lilies or other plants growing in the pool). One medium-sized water lily will provide sufficient shade for a 4- to 5-foot pool surface, and the floating leaves will help control the algae.

Visit water gardens for ideas as you plan your informal pool. Consult a pool supplier at a good nursery center before you purchase fish, snails, pumps, and filters.

Formal Pool

A FORMAL POOL is the "eye" of a formal garden. A carefully designed feature, it focuses attention but does not detract from other garden elements. For example, a circular pool with a fountain, placed in the center of a rose garden, is but one of many features in the landscape that balance and complement each other: box hedges surrounding the roses, rose beds of equal size, paths around the beds and pool, and arches for climbing roses and other plants at the entrance to the garden. To be effective, the pool must maintain the symmetry already established in the landscape.

You can use any preformed shape for your formal pool, but a circle (for example, 4 to 5 feet in diameter and 18 inches deep) is both classic and striking. Make certain your prefabricated mold is precise; round

Classic formality is achieved in this rose garden with a circular pool, a fountain, and symmetrical brick paths. Design by Ezra Haggard.

pools should be round. If you outline your pool with bricks or stones, be sure they are the same texture and color as those used in other parts of the garden.

Underwater lights are a common feature in both formal and informal pools. Dramatic scenes throwing falling water into relief against the darkness can be created using lights that are sealed and completely safe. Moderation is the key; too little is better than too much. Avoid colored lights, which can turn your pool into a floating circus.

Although a formal pool is primarily a reflecting pool, a fountain can add a delightful dimension. The height of the fountain jet should be no higher than one-half the diameter of the pool.

If you want to install a fountain or lights, consult a licensed electrician. Drill for wires before you sink your preformed pool.

Materials

A preformed fiberglass pool

Special Tools

Builder's level
One 2x4 the width of the pool

1. Place the preformed pool upside down, and use a spade to outline its circumference.

2. Dig out the sod and soil. Be sure to allow for the overhanging lip of the pool form (this area will not be excavated). Make the cavity slightly broader and deeper than the prefabricated pool form.

FORMAL POOL

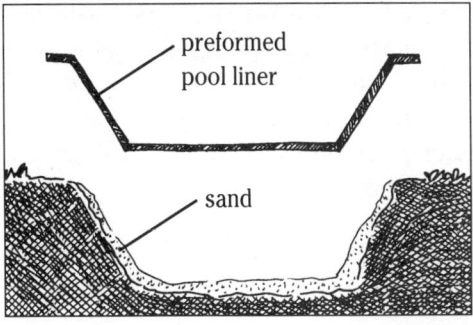

3. With moistened sand, pack the sides and bottom of the cavity. Make sure there is enough sand to support the mold.

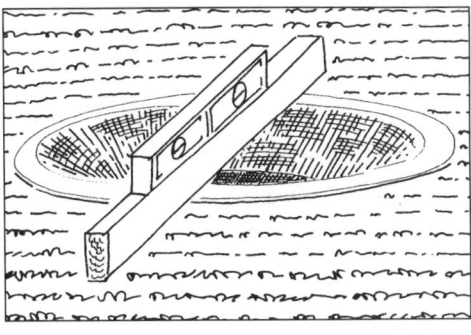

4. Insert the mold, then use a 2x4 and builder's level to determine whether the pool is level. If necessary, adjust the mold until all sides are level.

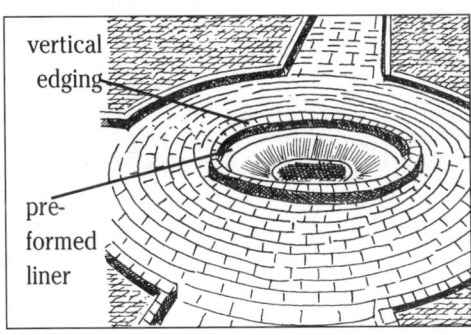

5. Sink vertical bricks around the lip of the pool, leaving one-third of the bricks exposed.

Suggested Plantings

Formal pools demand fewer plants than do informal pools; the many edging or underwater plants used with an informal pool are out of place in a formal design. If chosen to conform to the overall design, however, containerized plants make attractive accessories around the edge of a formal pool. You can even remove bricks or stones around the pool's circumference to make planting pockets. Just remember to exercise restraint, and pay close attention to size, color, and blooming season. For example, pots of spring bulbs can add patches of bright color early in the year, lilies during the summer, and chrysanthemums in the fall.

If you design a series of geometric beds surrounded by clipped box (*Buxus* spp.), try placing your pool in the center and planting the beds with herbs, roses, and bulbs. Paths leading to and from the pool will further define the patterns of each complementary bed. Again, be aware of color, height, and overall symmetry. Avoid masking the precise stone or brick outline of the pool with heavy plantings.

15

Cascading Water

Water cascades over a large stone along the edge of a shady natural pool. Maidenhair ferns surround and conceal the source of the water. Design by Ezra Haggard.

ONE OF THE EXQUISITE DELIGHTS of a garden is the sound of water. The soft, splashing sounds of cascading water refresh the spirit and help obliterate the noise of nearby traffic and other unpleasant urban sounds. Indeed, research indicates that the sound of running water is charged with negative ions that affect the human brain, producing a feeling of contentment.

If you don't have a running stream or natural water source on your property, you can easily create one. With careful construction, for example, you can create a stream of water falling over a stone, or a series of tiny streams appearing from under a stone ledge and cascading to your pool below.

Materials

Several large stones (see photograph and illustrations)
Pump to recirculate water
Flexible plastic hose (long enough to run from a submerged pump to the water source)

1. Hire a licensed electrician to install an outlet near your pool site. Select the location for your cascading water, and place large stones in a step arrangement. The stones should blend with other edging material. Tilt them slightly downward so that water will not flow behind them.

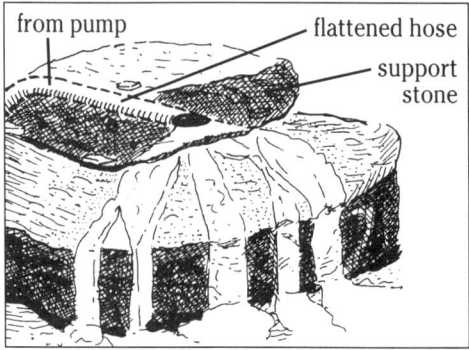

2. Conceal a flexible plastic hose under the stones. Place the open end under a rock at the top of the steps. The water should flow smoothly downward, over the stones, onto the surface of the pool below.

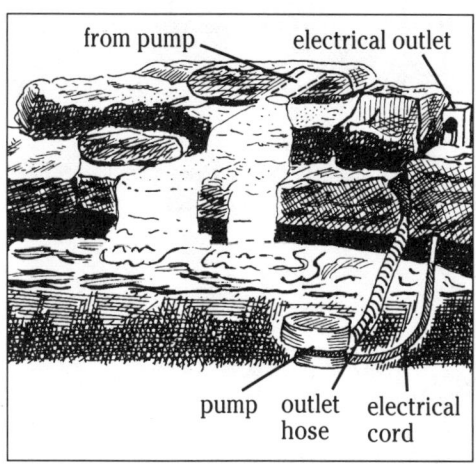

3. Place the pump at the bottom of the pool. Carefully arrange the stones and plants to conceal the hose carrying the water from the pump, as well as the electric cord (which powers the pump) running to the outlet.

Suggested Plantings

If your cascading water is located in the shade, plant ferns indigenous to your region. Several hardy species include Christmas fern *(Polystichum acrostichoides)*, lady fern *(Athyrium filix-femina)*, Japanese painted fern (*Athyrium goeringianum* 'Pictum'), or maidenhair fern *(Adiantum pedatum)*. Royal fern *(Osmunda regalis)* flourishes near water and is tall, vigorous, and graceful. For splashes of color, plant annual impatiens among or near your ferns.

For a sunny location, grasses are a perfect complement to falling water and are suitable for disguising electrical cords and outlets. Two of the smaller varieties (about 16 inches high) include the golden *Carex* 'Bowles Golden' and *Carex conica* 'Hime Kansuge', which has creamy white blades with green stripes.

Houttuynia cordata is very attractive near water. It produces dark green, heart-shaped leaves edged with red tones and splashes of cream. The red coloration is especially distinctive if the plant is grown in full sun. The leaves smell like Seville oranges when crushed. Because *H. cordata* is invasive, it should be planted in containers.

Japanese water iris *(Iris laevigata)* bears sword–shaped leaves and is beautiful with or without flowers. The blooming period is only a brief two to three weeks in spring, before the water lilies appear. Plant 'Midnight' (deep velvety-blue flowers), 'Rose Queen' (soft pink blooms), or 'Snowdrift' (snow–white flowers streaked with light blue).

For additional planting suggestions, check with your local nursery. Buy plants indigenous to your region, unless you can bring them into a garage or basement during the winter.

16

Formal Fountain

A formal pool with underwater lights and a multi-tiered fountain sits in the center of a rose garden. The paths surrounding the pool are edged in the ell-shaped brick pattern. Design by Ezra Haggard.

FORMAL FOUNTAIN

A SINGLE JET of water rising from the center of a classic circular pool is the exclamation point, the punctuation of a formal garden design. The sound is mesmerizing, and the patterns of sprays and ripples on the surface give us a feeling of well-being.

Decide on the type of fountain you want when you purchase your fiberglass pool or liner; the two must be compatible in scale. Be sure the size of your fountain conforms with the scale of your garden, and keep the design simple. A water jet should be in perfect harmony with the rest of the landscape.

If a single water jet isn't suitable, try a fountain sculpture. Garden centers sell many affordable designs made from precast materials with colored coatings. Lead and bronze fountains are expensive, but the detailing is often far superior. Antique fountain sculptures create a unique picture of light and water and can be purchased from specialty dealers for a hefty price.

Fountain ornaments usually have a pipe running through them for carrying water from the submerged pump to the outlet. The electrical outlet should be installed by a licensed electrician.

Because gusts of wind can deflect the rising water and quickly empty the pool, it's important to adjust the height of the water to one-half the diameter of the pool. Control valves and built-in flow regulators are often attached to the pump.

Materials

Pump with a flow regulator
Vertical copper tubing (long enough to extend 2 inches above the water surface for a single jet)
A prefabricated fountain ornament
Plinth, available at a pool supplier

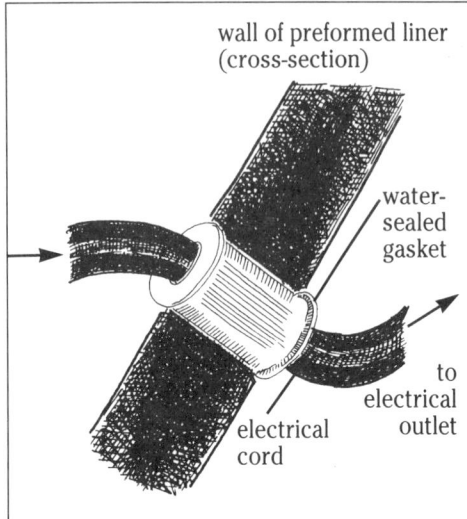

1. Run the electrical cord (for operating the pump) through the side of your fiberglass pool *before* you place the pool in its permanent location. Consult an electrician for this step.

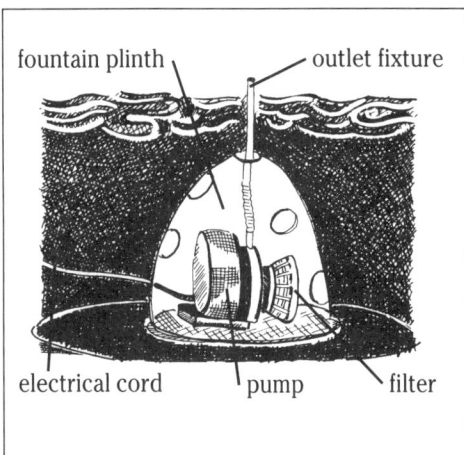

2. Place the fountain on a firm base in the center of the pool. If you are using a single jet, the device should protrude no more than 2 inches above the surface of the water. Secure the hose to the jet with a plinth. Some fountain ornaments come with a base; be sure to cushion it by using a large, flat, concrete slab on the bottom of the pool so you will not damage the liner.

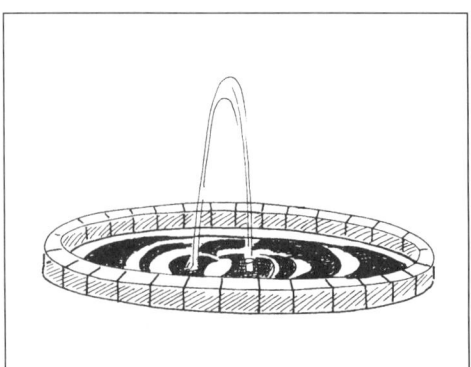

3. Adjust the height of the water (single jet or multijet) to one-half the diameter of the pool.

Garden Structures

17

Garden Screen

A GARDEN SCREEN is a practical and often necessary component of a landscape design that hides something we don't want to see—for example, pool filtration systems or central air-conditioning equipment. If it's attractive in its own right and provides additional growing space in the garden, it can also function as a decorative feature. For instance, a

*The rampant growth of the annual morning-glory (*Ipomoea *'Heavenly Blue') covers a garden screen positioned along a brick path.* Design by Ezra Haggard.

screen can provide a foil for low-growing shrubs and vertical space for climbers. It can also soften the area without creating a boxed-in feeling.

Always consider the color, height, and shape of your screen in relation to other garden structures. Painted or stained lattice will blend well with trellises, arbors, and privacy barriers elsewhere. Also keep in mind the space your screen will enclose and how it will affect the overall landscape design.

The following instructions are for building one screen 6 feet high and 4 feet wide. Be sure to use pressure-treated wood.

Materials

Two bags of ready-mix concrete
One bucket of coarse gravel (for drainage under posts)
Two 4x4s 8 feet long (for corner and end posts)
One 2x4 6 feet long
Two 2x4s 4 feet long (for bottom horizontals)
Two 2x4s approximately 60 inches long (for top horizontals)
One 2x4 2 feet long (for cross support)
Two 4x8 sheets of prefabricated lattice
Eight 1x½-inch 6-foot-long strips of wood
One box screw shank nails (size 12D)
One box finishing nails (size 3D)

Special Tools

Builder's level
Tape rule
Compass saw or jigsaw
Miter saw or miter box
Carpenter's steel square

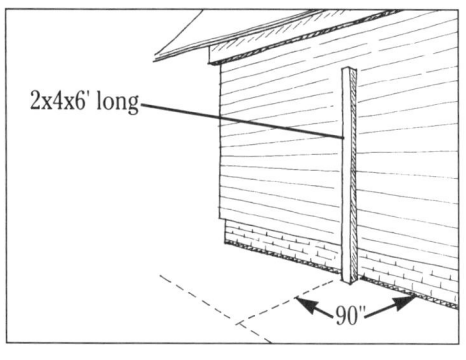

1. Nail one 6-foot 2x4 vertically to the building. Check the sides with a builder's level.

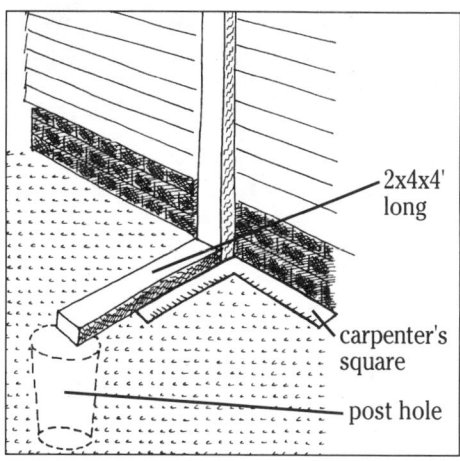

2. Place one 4-foot 2x4 on the ground perpendicular to the 6-foot 2x4 nailed to the building, and determine the location for the corner post hole. Position the base of a carpenter's steel square with the corner against the 2x4.

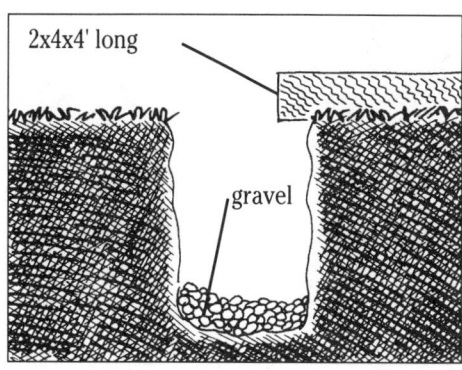

3. Dig the post hole 18–24 inches deep for positioning the corner post. Pour several inches of coarse gravel into the bottom of the post hole.

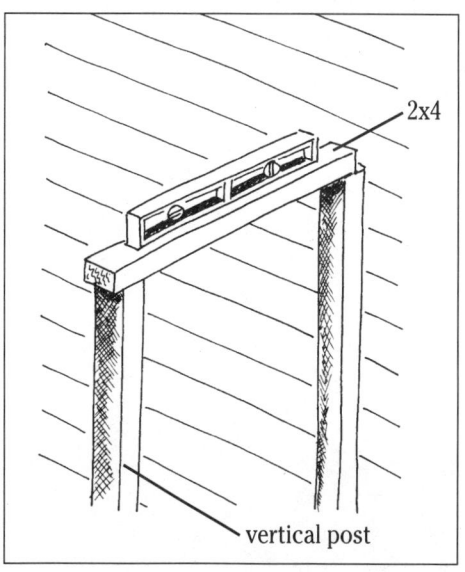

4. Check the measurements: the top of the corner post must be level with the top of the 2x4 nailed to the building. The corner post should be perpendicular to—and 4 feet from—the 2x4 nailed to the building.

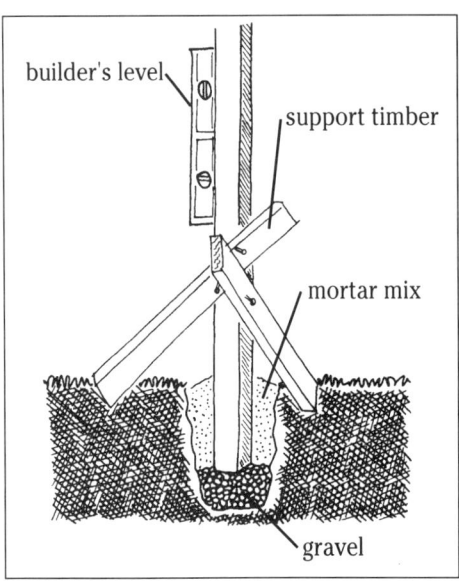

5. Position, brace, and level the corner post. Add ready-mix concrete.

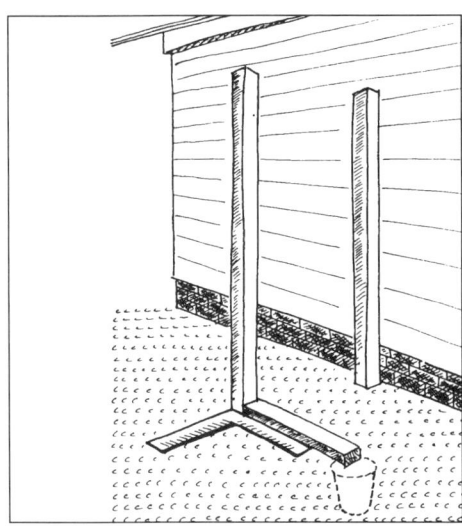

6. Place a carpenter's steel square against the corner post with the long side parallel to the building. Next, lay a 2x4 opposite the corner post and dig a second post hole. Install the second corner post.

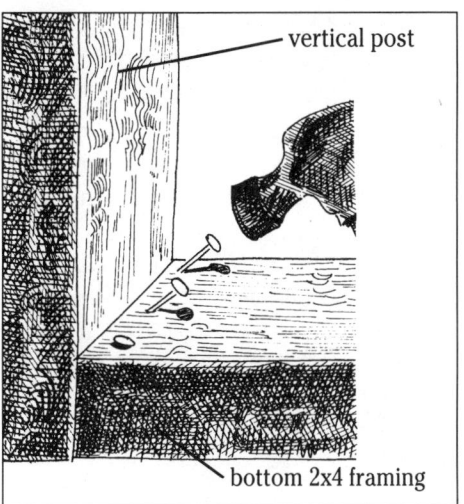

7. Toenail the bottom horizontal 2x4s into place.

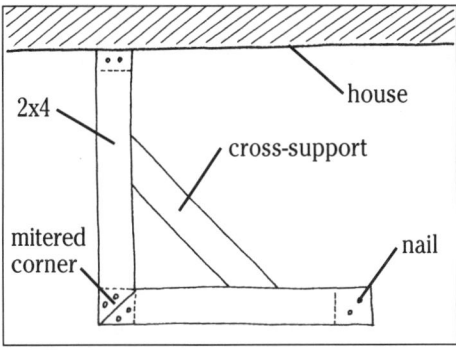

8. Miter the top 2x4 horizontals where they join at the corner post, as shown in the illustration. Nail into place the top horizontal 2x4s and cross brace.

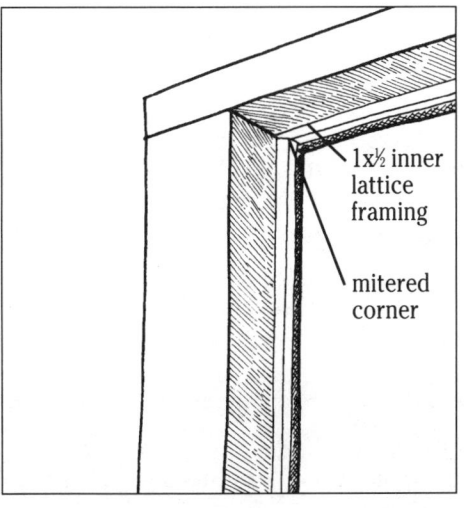

9. Cut and miter the outer set of framing strips for the lattice, and nail them into place with finishing nails (size 3D). These strips form the vertical framework for the two sheets of lattice.

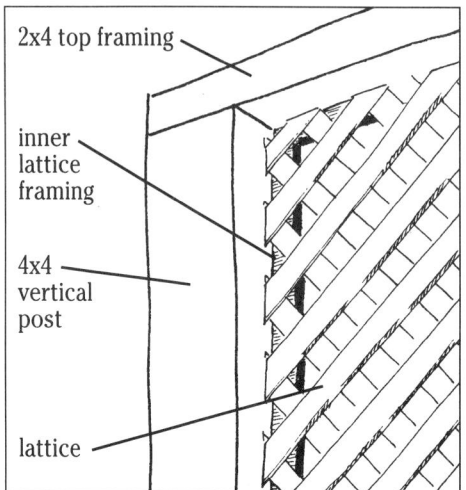

10. Cut two sheets of lattice to the exact size of the screen: measure inside from vertical 2x4 to vertical 2x4. Nail both sections of the lattice onto the outer framing strips already in place. These strips serve as a framework for your lattice sections. The lattice will be sandwiched between the outer and inner framing strips with mitered corners.

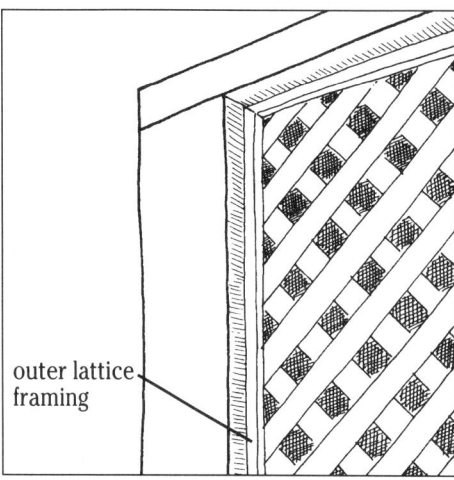

11. Miter, cut, and install the remaining framing strips. Paint or stain the screen.

Suggested Plantings

When selecting perennial or annual vines for a garden screen, consider their growth habits and light requirements. Tie your vines to the latticework as they grow. Clip wandering shoots before they encroach on what you are concealing behind your screen.

A suitable perennial vine for a sunny location is *Actinidia kolomikta*, which produces leaf tips blotched with pink and white. Its blooms appear early in the spring.

Try five-leaf akebia *(Akebia quinata)*, a fast-growing but graceful vine that will flourish in partial shade.

Porcelain vine *(Ampelosis brevipedunculata)* produces blue fruit that gradually turns to turquoise as it matures. The foliage is often variegated white and green.

Another hardy climber is American bittersweet *(Celastrus scandens)*, which bears tiny spring flowers and clusters of fall fruit that can be dried for indoor arrangements. It thrives in ordinary garden soil and light shade.

Japanese hops *(Humulus japonicus* 'Variegatus') is also a good choice for garden screens. It offers lacquer-green leaves washed in white.

Suitable annual vines include morning-glory *(Ipomoea tricolor)*. For a more exotic look, try *I. imperialis* 'Chocolate', which bears deep, brownish-red flowers, or *I. batatas* 'Blackie', a shy bloomer with deep black, glossy stems and purple-black foliage. If you can't find these varieties, the traditional *I.* 'Heavenly Blue' is always dependable.

If you plant sweet peas *(Lathyrus odoratus)*, stretch a piece of plastic pea netting the width of your screen 1 foot from ground level so that the tender vines can firmly attach themselves before climbing the lattice.

⟨18⟩

Privacy Barrier

A FENCE NEED NOT LOOK like a fence. If you decide to separate your shrub or herbaceous border from an adjoining property, you can build a barrier using wooden panels and lattice. The lattice will counteract the closed-in feeling one so often gets from privacy fences.

An open–style barrier not only is striking as a divider within the garden, but also visually sets off a particular area of the landscape—creating the illusion of space for even the smallest garden. Make your privacy barrier any length you want, but keep in mind that the border you create is an ideal opportunity for displaying seasonal color and architectural balance. Paint or stain the framework to blend with other garden features.

A privacy barrier composed of five panels separates a perennial border from the neighboring property. Silvery and spiky variegated grasses mixed with colorful annuals complement the lines and color of the structure. Design by Ezra Haggard.

PRIVACY BARRIER 105

The following materials are necessary for building one panel; for each additional panel you build, add one post and double the amount of materials. Buy pressure-treated lumber. The finial-topped posts and scalloped board can be purchased ready-made.

Materials

Two 4x4-inch posts 8½ feet long with pyramidal finial tops
Three 2x8-inch boards 10 feet long
One 2x12-inch scalloped board, 8 feet 8½ inches long
Three 1x¾-inch strips, 8 feet long
One 4x8 sheet of prefabricated small-hole lattice
Four bags of ready-mix concrete
One 5-gallon bucket of crushed gravel
One box of screw shank nails (size 12D)
One box of finishing nails (size 4D)

Special Tools

Builder's level
Line level
Tape rule
Jigsaw and circular power saw
Several pieces of scrap 2x4s

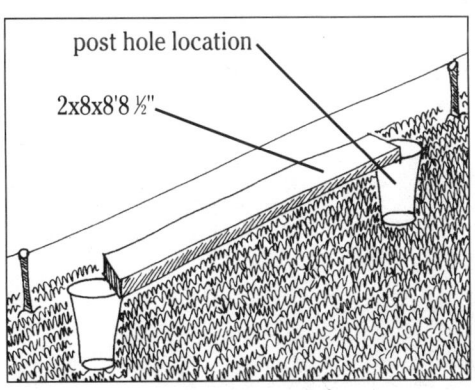

1. Select a level piece of ground for your privacy barrier. Stretch a string between two stakes on your property line. Lay one 2x8-inch board (cut 8 feet 8½ inches long) on the ground and dig a post hole at each end, 24 inches deep. Fill each hole with 6 inches of crushed gravel.

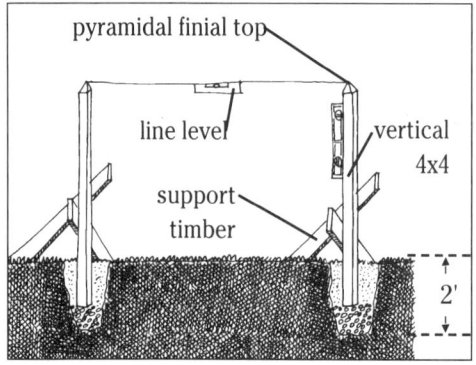

2. Sink the vertical posts. Brace each post, check with a builder's level, and adjust accordingly. Use a line level suspended between the two posts to be sure each post is the same height. Pour concrete into the hole and let it cure.

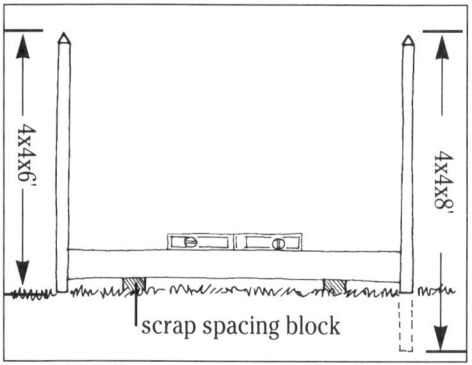

3. Draw a line down the center of each post. Position a 2x8–inch board (cut 8 feet 8 ½ inches long) at the bottom for toenailing. Place support blocks (scrap 2x4s) under the 2x8 and check the top with a builder's level.

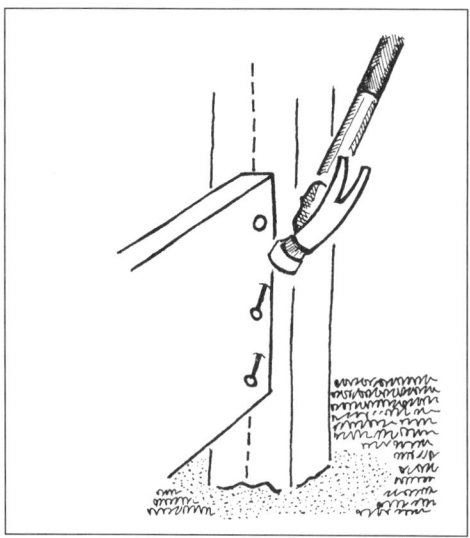

4. Toenail the 2x8 into place along the center line.

PRIVACY BARRIER

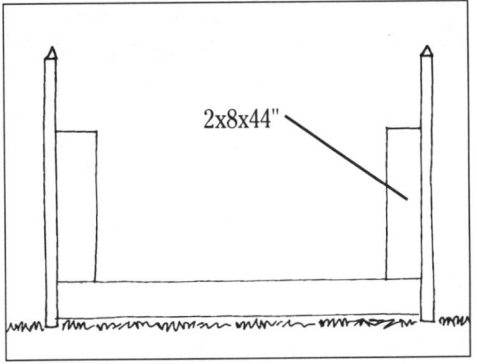

5. Following the vertical line down the center of each post, toenail the left and right vertical 2x8s (cut 3 feet 8 inches long) into place.

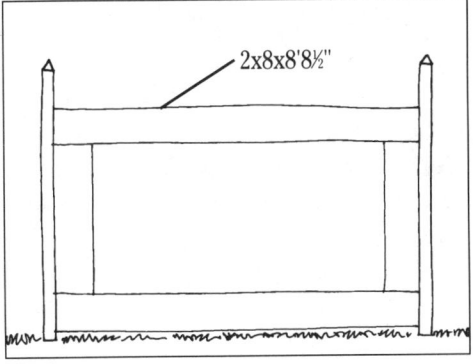

6. Toenail the top 2x8 (cut 8 feet 8½ inches long) securely into place.

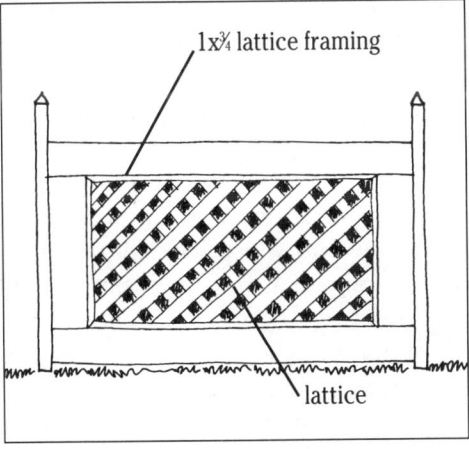

7. Cut the lattice sheet to fit the opening (approximately 7 feet, 5 inches long by 3 feet, 8 inches high). Cut the 1x3/4–inch strips to match the length and width of the sheet of lattice. Nail the lattice into place using the framing strips and size 4D finishing nails. The lattice will be sandwiched between the strips. For a more finished appearance, miter the strips.

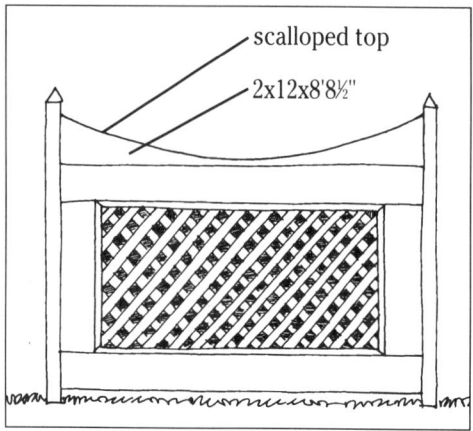

8. On top of the lattice-framed panel, toenail into place the scalloped 2x12-inch board (cut 8 feet 8 inches long). Paint or stain the panel.

Suggested Plantings

A good color to paint your privacy barrier is peppercorn black—a blend of equal amounts of flat green and flat black. A black barrier makes a handsome backdrop for the interweaving of branches, stems, leaves, and flowers in your border.

Before planting anything in front of your barrier, prepare the soil and check for adequate drainage. Purchase the best plants available, and buy a dozen of one variety so that you can mass them for effect.

For a colorful combination of pink, purple, silver, green, and yellow, plant a smokebush (*Cotinus coggygria* 'Royal Purple') at one corner of the barrier. In front of the smokebush, use three clumps of the ivory- and green-striped variegated yucca *(Yucca filamentosa)*. Surrounding the base of the yuccas, plant a ground cover, such as the clump-forming ajuga (*Ajuga* 'Metallica Crispa'). Off center, use a dozen plantings of *Geranium* 'Johnson's Blue' interplanted with *Artemisia* 'Powis Castle'.

A perfect rose for the trellis is the thornless, cerise-pink *Rosa* 'Zéphirine Drouhin'; it is free-flowering, strongly scented, and disease-free. Try training clematis to intertwine with the canes. *Clematis* 'Niobe', which has blood-red blooms and gold stamens, or the white 'Huldine' or 'Candide' are good choices.

At the opposite end of the border, use *Viburnum plicatum* 'Mariesii', a white, lace-cap cultivar.

In front of the viburnum, plant three barberries (*Berberis thunbergii* 'Rose Glow'). Their tiny wine-colored foliage will complement the larger satin-purple leaves of the smokebush on the other end.

In front of the barberries and along the edge of the border, use lady's-mantle *(Alchemilla mollis)* for its leaf texture, yellow-green color, and scallop-shaped leaves.

For contrast, add clumps of coralbells (*Heuchera* 'Palace Purple'). In the center-front portion of the border, try a patch of lamb's-ears (*Stachys byzantina* 'Silver Carpet'), dwarf black mondo grass (*Ophiopgon planiscapus* 'Nigrescens'), and *Ajuga* 'Burgundy Glow'. This arrangement will continue the theme of silver, cream, pink, and purple.

White is important because it suggests space and creates contrasts; nearby colors seem richer and more vibrant. For an attractive spring and summer display, plant white delphiniums, foxglove, and lilies in the back of the border. Don't forget *Baptisia leucantha*, which produces tall black stems, semi-waxy foliage, and a profusion of pure white, pealike blooms.

These selections will provide a year-round display of complementary colors in front of your black privacy barrier. They will cover every inch of your border if they receive at least half a day of sunlight.

A Freestanding Arbor

IMAGINE A PLEASANT SPOT in the summer where you can sit in the cool shade and catch the scent of flowers nearby. Around you, luxuriant climbers form a dense arcade, rambling up the sides and spilling over the roof beams. You reach up and nibble from a hanging cluster of grapes.

A freestanding arbor provides shade as well as a place for relaxing and viewing the garden. It can also add a new dimension to the landscape. Built at the end of a path, for example, it becomes a secluded outdoor room; placed at or near the center of the garden, it serves as a link

---

A garden arbor is framed with a grape vine and sweet autumn clematis (Clematis paniculata). Boxwood and quince grow on each side of the entrance. Patches of lamb's-ears form silver pools that contrast with the peppercorn black of the structure. Design by Ezra Haggard.

A FREESTANDING ARBOR

between areas. As with any garden structure, it's important to balance the overall look and size of the arbor with other features in the landscape.

The following instructions are for building a freestanding arbor 9 feet high, 12 feet long, and 5 feet wide. Be sure to buy pressure-treated lumber.

Materials

Four 4x4-inch posts, 11 feet long
Eight 2x4s, 8 feet long
Four 2x4s, 6 feet long
Four 2x4s, 4 feet long (for end horizontals)
Nine 2x6-inch boards, 12 feet long (for top)
Three 2x8-inch boards, 10 feet long (front, back, and end crossbeams)
One 4x8 sheet of prefabricated small-hole lattice
One box of 4-inch galvanized wood screws
Five 1x3/4-inch strips, 8 feet long *or* four 6 feet long and one 8 feet long
Eight bags of ready-mix concrete
Three buckets of crushed gravel

Special Tools

Builder's level
Carpenter's steel square
Butt chisel
One pound box of screw shank nails (size 16D)
One box 3-inch wood screws
¼ pound of finishing nails (size 3D)
Tape rule
Circular power saw
Jigsaw (for lattice)
Electric drill

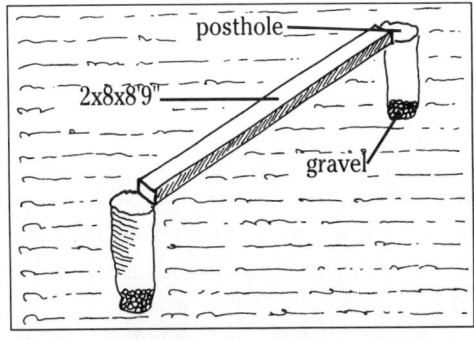

1. Lay one 2x8 board (cut to 8 feet 9 inches long) on the ground where you intend to build the arbor. Dig a post hole at each end, 30 inches deep. Add 6 inches of crushed gravel to each hole.

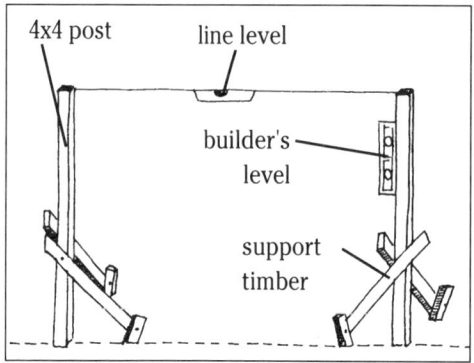

2. Sink and brace the two posts. Check the sides with a builder's level and the tops with a line level. Fill the holes with ready-mix concrete.

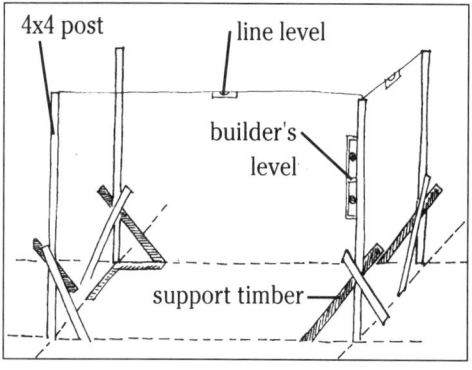

3. Using a carpenter's steel square, position a 4-foot 2x4 perpendicular to each post. Dig holes at each end of the 2x4s and repeat steps 1 and 2. Make certain all posts are vertical to one another and that all tops are level.

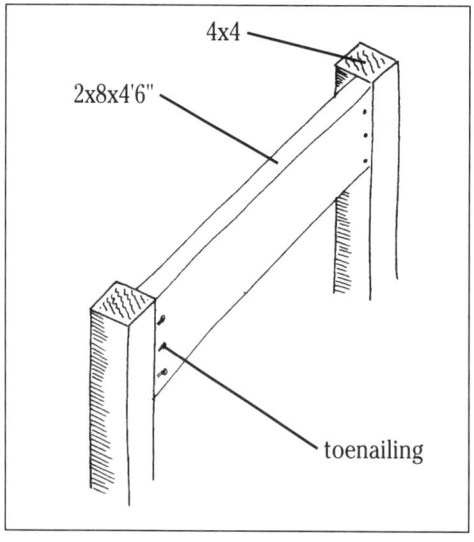

4. Install the cross braces (2x6s cut 4 feet 6 inches long). Toenail them lightly into place.

A FREESTANDING ARBOR

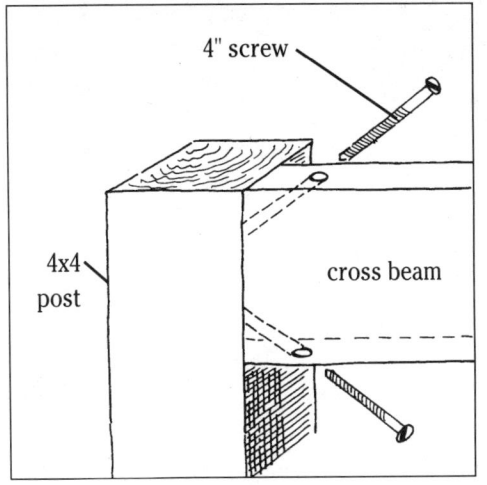

5. For each cross brace, drill four holes for wood screws at approximately 45–degree angles through each corner. Be sure to drill only through the cross braces and not into the posts. The holes should be slightly larger than the screws. Sink the screws and remove the nails (used for toenailing) from the cross braces. Repeat the same procedure for the opposite end of the arbor.

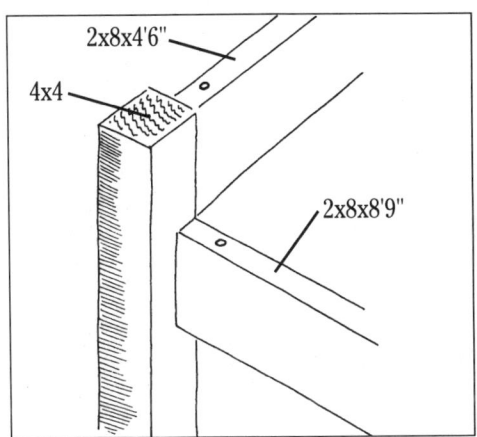

6. To install the front and back cross beams (2x8x8'9"), repeat steps 4 and 5.

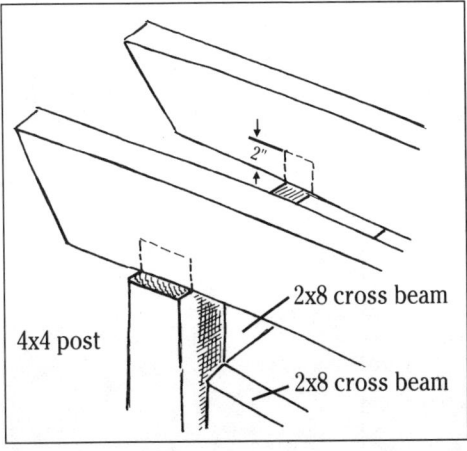

7. Miter the ends of all eight 2x6x12–foot cross beams at 60–degree angles. Mark the two front and back cross beams that will fit across the tops of the four posts. Mark the six inner cross beams (2x6x12) that will form the roof of the arbor, as shown in the illustration.

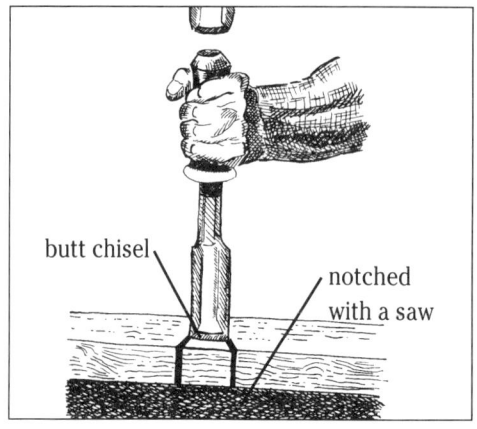

8. Following the marks on all cross beams, make two cuts 2 inches deep (use a circular power saw). Using a butt chisel and a hammer, cut out notches.

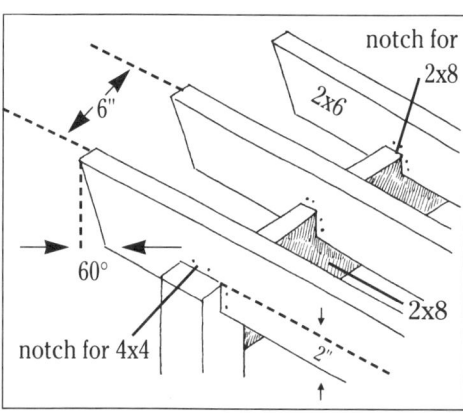

9. Toenail into position the roof beams on both sides of the arbor. Space equally, approximately 6 inches apart.

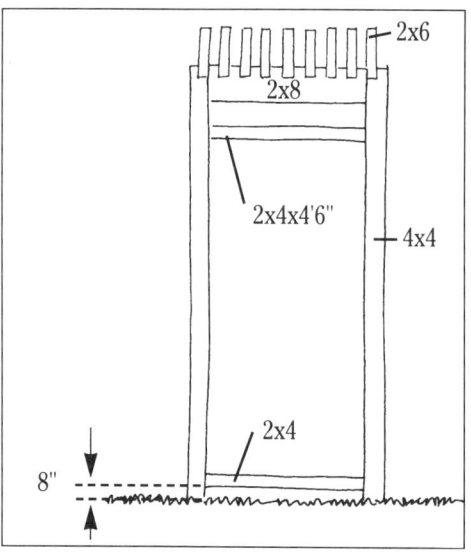

10. Toenail the bottom horizontal 2x4, 8 inches from ground level. Install the second horizontal 2x4 6 feet above the bottom 2x4. Repeat the same procedure for the opposite end of the arbor.

A FREESTANDING ARBOR

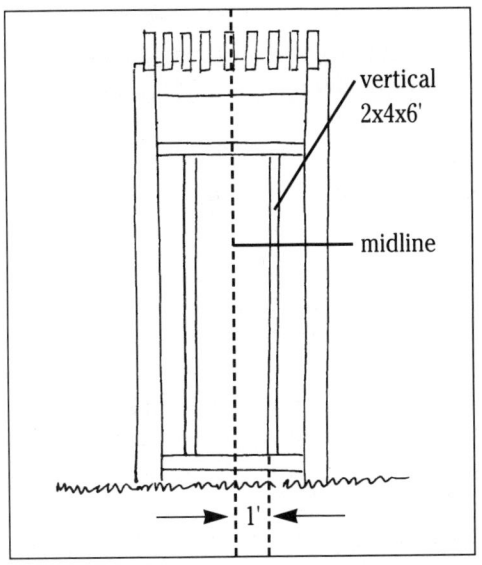

11. Install the vertical 2x4s to fit between the horizontal 2x4s, and space each board 1 foot from the center lines on the posts.

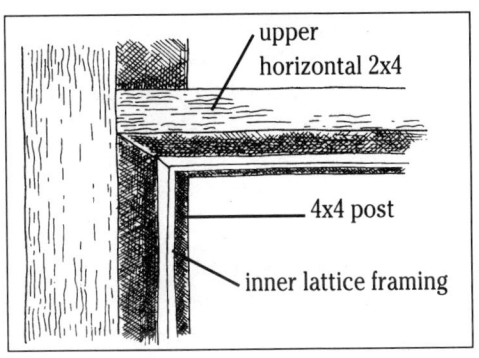

12. Construct a framework using mitered 1x¾–inch strips. Attach one set of framing strips using finishing nails (size 3D).

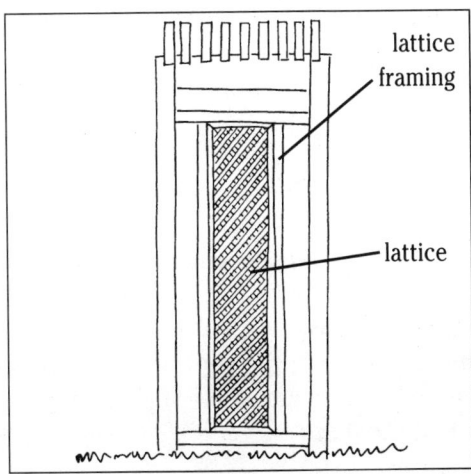

13. Following the center lines on each post, install the lattice panel (cut 2x6 feet). Attach the second set of mitered framing strips using finishing nails (size 3D). Repeat the same procedure for the opposite end of the arbor. When the arbor is completed, paint or stain it or, if you wish, allow the pressure–treated wood to weather naturally.

Suggested Plantings

Before planting, dig the soil deeply and add compost, Canadian sphagnum peat moss, and well-rotted manure. To ensure good drainage, mix a few shovelfuls of pea gravel into your beds.

Use your arbor to support climbers, and plant complementary perennials and shrubs around it. The following plants will provide complementary seasonal colors in shades of green, red, pink, yellow, and white.

A grape vine (*Vitis* spp.) growing up one corner of an arbor is strong enough to support a delicate climber such as *Clematis* 'Gravetye Beauty', which bears ruby–red flowers in autumn, or the more diminutive yellow–flowering *Clematis* 'Tangutica'.

Vitis 'Interlaken' is a yellowish green, almost seedless table grape that is suitable for growing in the Midwest, North, and Northeast. It grows well in an arbor and is a tasty treat. Gardeners in California and the Northwest could plant the cherry-red *Vitis* 'Cardinal', a very productive table grape that flourishes in hot areas, including some parts of the Southwest. Another satisfactory green grape for growing in these areas is *Vitis* 'Thompson Seedless'. With the exception of Muscadine varieties grown in the South, most grapes don't need to be cross–pollinated.

Plant a variety of honeysuckle, such as *Lonicera periclymenum* var. *belgica*, for early-spring flowers, or the autumn–blooming *L. periclymenum* var. *serotina*. Both have a strong scent. Since the lower portions of honeysuckle vines often become unsightly as the season progresses, it's a good idea to include clumps of flowering perennials to hide the bare vines. If the sun isn't too strong and there is adequate moisture, *Hosta* 'Honeybells' or 'Royal Standard' make good camouflage. The foliage is dramatic in both texture and shape; the lavender and white flowers are sweetly scented.

Be wary of wisterias: they produce lovely racemes of spring flowers, but the vines cover a structure with a pythonlike tenacity. If you don't have the time or energy to keep an eye on their rapid growth, they will severely damage your arbor.

Climbing roses are striking on an arbor. The bright yellow *Rosa* 'Golden Showers' is ideal; its semi-double blooms appear throughout the summer and fall, and are exquisite against a black framework.

For twining through the canes of a yellow rose, plant *Clematis viticella* 'Betty Corning'. The beautiful smoky-blue, bell–shaped flowers bloom concurrently with *Rosa* 'Golden Showers'.

If you want quick results while the more permanent climbers establish themselves, sow seeds of annual vines such as morning–glory (*Ipomoea* 'Heavenly Blue') or sweet pea (*Lathyrus odoratus*).

Formal Rose Garden with Brick Paths and Fountain

IF YOU HAVE a large, flat expanse of lawn that requires constant mowing—and if the area is located in full sun and has no encroaching tree roots—consider planting a formal rose garden. Such a garden brings welcome order to a chaotic world and nourishes the human spirit with calming elements: the sight and fragrance of colorful, exquisitely shaped blooms; the ordered charm of neat paths; the sound of falling water; or the movement of a leaf on the surface of a circular pool.

Sit down with a sheet of graph paper and draw a plan. Decide on the size of your beds, the shape of the paths, and the roses and complementary plantings required. Keep in mind that a successful formal rose

The brick paths have been constructed and the rosebeds laid out; a fountain will form the focus of this formal garden. Design by Ezra Haggard.

garden is a structured plan, precisely measured and carefully planted. Study books with pictures of rose gardens from the past, or better yet, visit gardens for inspiration.

The following instructions are for building a formal rose garden measuring 46 feet by 37 feet.

Materials

Graph paper
Bricks or stones (selected to match others in the landscape)
A piece of 2x4
Builder's sand (order 2 cubic yards from a stone center)
Pulverized limestone
Circular preformed pool
Pump and fountain

Special Tools

Rubber mallet
Tape rule
Cold chisel
Circular power saw with masonry blade (for cutting bricks, if necessary)

1. Draw a plan on graph paper using a scale of ⅛ inch for 1 foot. Indicate the perimeters of the entire garden (beginning with the ell-shaped brick edging), the inner rose beds (parterres), and the formal pool area, as well as the width and length of the paths.

FORMAL ROSE GARDEN

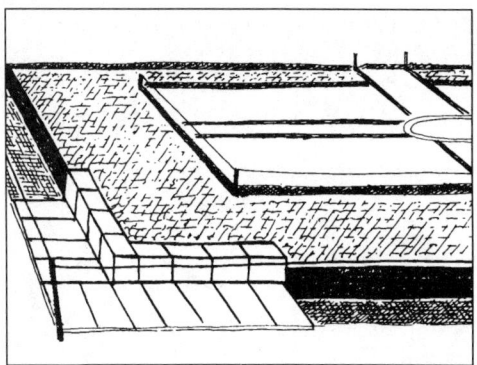

2. Using stakes, string, and a garden hose, lay out the design of the garden. Dig trenches for the ell-shaped brick edging. (See Chapter One for more on brick edging.)

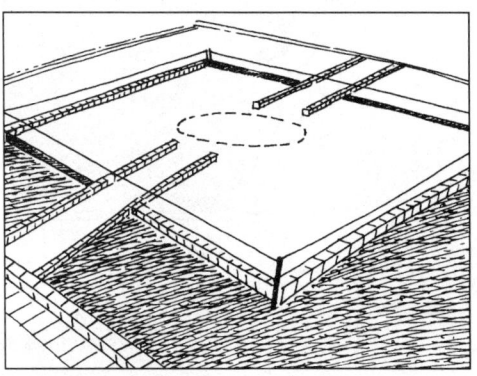

3. Following the string and stake outlines, install vertical bricks to frame the parterres. Install a formal pool and fountain, then install ell–shaped bricks around the pool. (See Chapters Fourteen and Sixteen for more on formal pools and fountains.)

4. Excavate areas for walks up to and around the circular pool, and lay the bricks. (See Chapter Two for more on brick paths.) Install a circular brick pattern around the pool.

1. *R.* 'Baroness Rothschild'
2. *R.* 'Boule de Neige'
3. *R.* 'Baroness Rothschild'
4. *R. gallica officinalis*
5. *R.* 'Golden Wings'
6. *R.* 'Léda'
7. *R.* 'Golden Wings'
8. *R.* 'Comte de Chambord'
9. *R.* 'Zéphirine Drouhin'
10. *R.* 'Lilian Austin'
11. *R.* 'Fantin Latour'
12. *R.* 'Tuscany'
13. *R.* 'Heritage'
14. *R.* 'Belle Isis'
15. *R.* 'Belle Isis'
16. *R.* 'Gruss an Aachen'
17. *R.* 'Gruss an Aachen'
18. *R.* 'Gruss an Aachen'
19. *R.* 'Zéphirine Drouhin'

FORMAL ROSE GARDEN

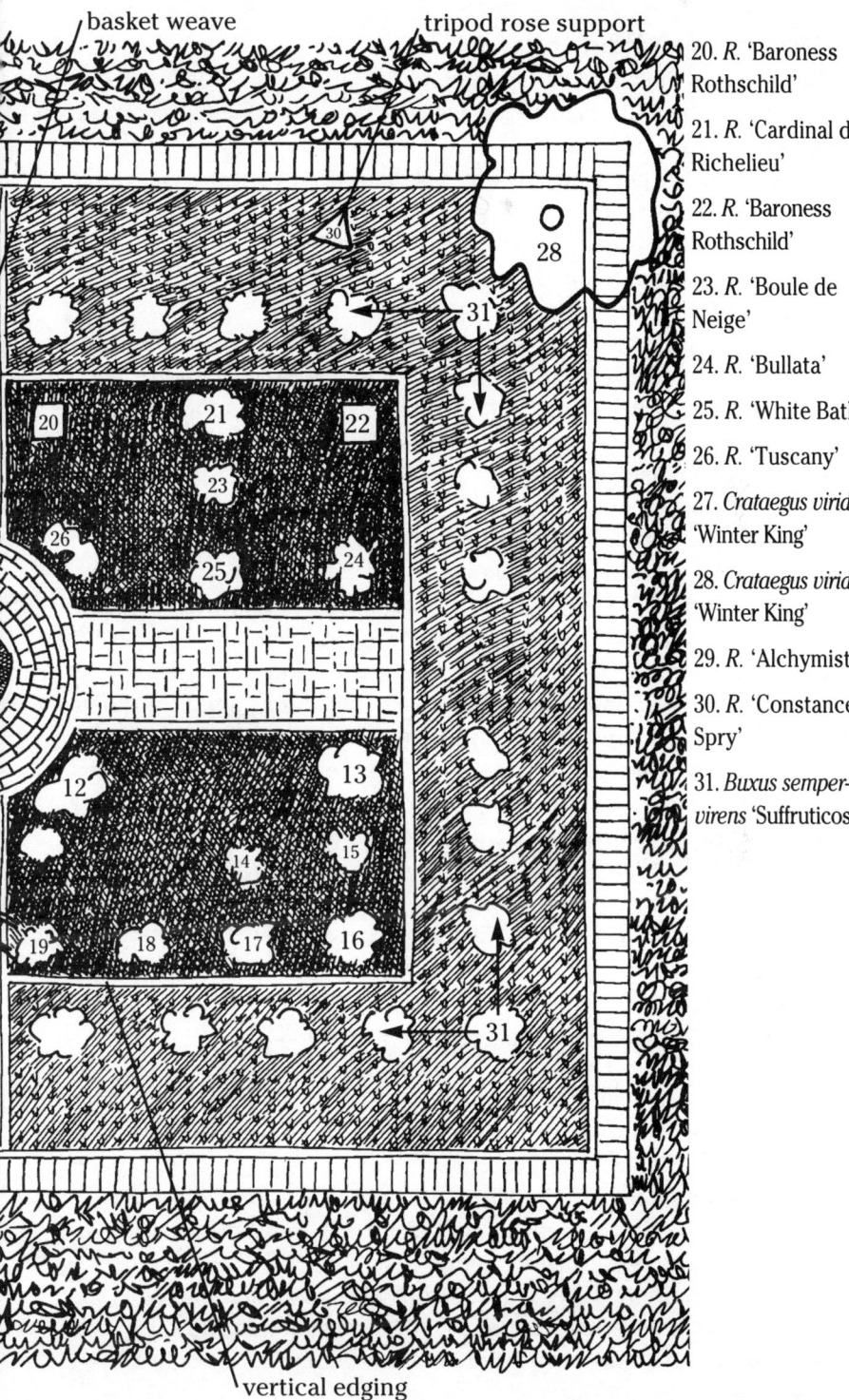

basket weave
tripod rose support
vertical edging

20. *R.* 'Baroness Rothschild'
21. *R.* 'Cardinal de Richelieu'
22. *R.* 'Baroness Rothschild'
23. *R.* 'Boule de Neige'
24. *R.* 'Bullata'
25. *R.* 'White Bath'
26. *R.* 'Tuscany'
27. *Crataegus viridis* 'Winter King'
28. *Crataegus viridis* 'Winter King'
29. *R.* 'Alchymist'
30. *R.* 'Constance Spry'
31. *Buxus sempervirens* 'Suffruticosa'

Suggested Rose Plantings

Prepare the soil in each rose bed by incorporating generous quantities of Canadian sphagnum peat moss, well-rotted manure, and pea gravel (if the soil is heavy clay).

Surrounding the perimeter of the rose beds—between the ell-shaped brick edging defining the entire garden and the vertical edging within—plant boxwood (*Buxus sempervirens* 'Suffruticosa'). Box lends itself to clipping and pruning, and its symmetry defines the four rose parterres that form the geometric design.

When selecting your roses, consider the color, the variety, and the ultimate height and spread of each plant. There are old–fashioned varieties (popular in the nineteenth century) as well as modern roses (hybrid teas, floribundas, grandifloras, climbers, and miniatures).

In the garden illustrated are the following roses:

Bed One

'Baroness Rothschild' (1868) is a large, soft, double pink-rose. The bush explodes with blooms early in the season.

'Boule de Neige' (1867) is a very fragrant, double white rose that blooms throughout the summer. Its foliage is a dark green.

Rosa gallica officinalis—sometimes called the "Apothecary Rose"—is an ancient rose. It is almost thornless and produces small purplish-crimson clusters of flowers early in the season.

'Golden Wings' (1956) is a modern shrub rose with large flowers that are single or semi-double and lightly scented. It blooms over a long period beginning in early June. There are two plants of 'Golden Wings' in this garden plan.

Bed Two

'Léda' (prior to 1827) is a painted damask rose; milk-white blooms are edged with crimson. The plant produces downy, gray–green foliage.

'Fantin Latour' (date unknown) is a pale shell-pink, highly fragrant shrub rose. Its foliage is also gray-green. It is thought to have been a favorite with old Dutch and Flemish painters.

'Lilian Austin' is a modern shrub rose that produces salmon–pink flowers tinged with apricot. It grows into a low, arching mound and has a good record of flowering repeatedly.

'Comte de Chambord' (c. 1860) is a bright, warm pink double rose with a quartered petal arrangement. It blooms in mid-June and is highly scented, but is a one–time bloomer.

'Zéphirine Drouhin' (1868) is a vigorous shrub or climbing rose (see photograph) that will cover an arch in one season. It is thornless and produces large clusters of semi–double flowers that are a bright cerise-pink. Because of its strong scent, it is ideal for training on an arch or cascading over an arbor. Two plants of 'Zéphirine Drouhin' appear in this plan—one on each side of the arch.

Bed Three

'Tuscany Superb' (a sport of 'Tuscany' that occurred in England prior to 1848) is a magnificent rose in full bloom: its deep maroon-crimson flowers contrast well with the light green foliage. It blooms only once during the season.

'Heritage' is a modern English shrub rose with many characteristics common to the old-fashioned roses: clear, shell–pink double blooms with a cupped shape, a strong lemon fragrance, and robust growth to 4 feet. It will bloom all season.

'Belle Isis' (1845) is a pure flesh-pink with white edges and ideally suited to the small garden. Its ultimate height is about 3 feet. There are two plants in this bed.

'Gruss an Aachen' (1909) occupies three spots in this bed, and rightly so; the creamy–pink flowers of this low-growing rose are highly fragrant and will bloom all season. There are three plants in this bed.

Bed Four

'Cardinal de Richelieu' (1840) is a popular, old Gallica rose with velvet-purple blooms that appear in clusters. As the blooms age, they turn a slate-mauve color that is a striking contrast to other blooms in the garden. It flowers only once a season but puts on a lavish production.

'Tuscany' and 'Baroness Rothschild' are also included in this bed (see Beds One and Three).

'White Bath' (1810) is sometimes listed as *R. centifolia muscosa alba*. The double white flowers have a green eye. The shrub grows in an open fashion and is highly fragrant.

'Bullata' (1815) is sometimes listed as the "Lettuce Leaf Rose." It is one of the few roses that are better known for their foliage than their flowers. It produces large, distinctively veined leaves. The medium pink, double flowers are stunning with the foliage.

Tripod Supports

'Alchymist' is a vigorous plant that bears orange–peach blossoms and dark green, glossy foliage tinged with bronze. It flowers profusely from spring to early summer.

'Constance Spry' (1961) is a vigorous shrub or pillar rose—ideal for growing on a tripod support. The flowers are myrrh–scented, deep pink, well-formed, and double. It blooms only once a season, but its arching canes give an impressive performance.

Suggested Complementary Plantings

You can simply mulch your rose beds with shredded pine bark chips (an ideal color) and focus exclusively on the boxwood, rose bushes, pool, fountain, and geometric patterns of your formal parterres. Or you can add ground covers, which—when planted in moderation—will provide touches of color as the seasons pass.

Use these hardy plants to complement the roses when they are in bloom and—equally important—to provide distinctive foliage and flowers when some roses have finished their annual display. Avoid any underplantings that require deep cultivation, which would disturb the shallow roots of the roses.

Forget-me-nots *(Omphalodes verna)* will grow 8 inches tall and create a blue mist under roses in early summer.

Gray blends well with mauve and pink blooms; lamb's-ears *(Stachys byzantina)* provides a soft, silvery carpet under roses. You can also use this low-growing perennial as a border.

Chives, parsley, and Alpine strawberries are excellent ground covers or can be used as edging plants.

You can create a Persian carpet effect by blending the pink, purple, and mauve flowers of assorted varieties of thyme with the large, muted, soft shades of the roses. *Thymus x citriodorous* 'Aureus' is especially useful with dark red or yellow roses.

Basil is effective under pink roses, especially the dark opal *Ocimum basilicum*, which has almost black leaves. It grows approximately 16 inches high, so plant it with the taller rose varieties. Golden marjoram (*Origanum vulgare* 'Aureum') is striking with pink, yellow, or white roses.

For a sea of green, try lady's-mantle *(Alchemilla mollis)*; all roses benefit from its presence. The tiny sprays of chartreuse flowers are remarkable foils for pale pink, mauve, apricot, and red roses.

Sources of Supplies

Carroll Gardens
444 East Main Street
P.O. Box 310
Westminster, MD 21157

Foliage Gardens
Att: Sue Olsen
2003 128th Avenue SE
Bellevue, WA 98005

Lamb Nurseries
East 101 Sharp Avenue
Spokane, WA 99202

Lilypons Water Gardens
1626 Hort Road
P.O. Box 10
Lilypons, MD 21717-0010
or
1626 Lilypons Road
P.O. Box 188
Brookshire, TX 77423-0188

Pickering Nurseries, Inc.
670 Kingston Road (Hwy. 2)
Pickering, Ontario
Canada
(No plant import permit necessary)

Roses of Thomasville
Thomasville Nurseries
P.O. Box 7
Thomasville, GA 31799

Roses of Yesterday & Today
Brown's Valley Road
Watsonville, CA 95076-0398

Smith & Hawken
25 Corte Madera
Mill Valley, CA 94941-1829

Vick's Wildgardens
Box 115
Gladwyn, PA 19055

The Wayside Gardens Co.
Hodges, SC 29695

White Flower Farm
Litchfield, CT 06759

Index

Note: Italicized page numbers refer to material in illustrations and photographs.

Abronia spp. (sand verbena), 26
Acorus (sweet flag)
  A. calamus (common), 82
  A. gramineus (dwarf), 82
Actinidia kolomikta, 41, 102
Adiantum pedatum (maidenhair fern), 7, 66, *89,* 91
Aethionema 'Wendy Rose' (Persian candytuft), 71-72
Agave vilmoriniana (octopus agave), 26
Ajuga
  A. 'Burgundy Glow,' 60, 109
  A. 'Metallica Crispa,' 60, 108
Akebia quinata (five-leaf akebia), 102
Alchemilla mollis (lady's-mantle), 7, 109, 124
Allium cyaneum, 73
Alpine strawberry, 124
Alyssum condensatum, 73
American bittersweet. *See Celastrus scandens*
Ampelopsis brevipedunculata (porcelain vine), 46, 102
Androsace spp. (rock jasmine), 71, 73
Arabis spp. (rock cress), 73
Aristolochia durior (Dutchman's-pipe), 40-41
Armeria spp. (thrift), 72
arrowhead. *See Sagittaria* spp.
Artemisia 'Powis Castle,' 108
Arum italicum 'Pictum,' 25-26
Asplenium scolopendrium (harts-tongue fern), 66
Aster, 25
  A. novi-belgii (dwarf), 25
astilbe, 7

Athyrium
  A. filix-femina (lady fern), 91
  A. goeringianum 'Pictum' (Japanese painted fern), 91
Aubrieta deltoidea, 73
Aurinia, 73
  A. saxatilis 'Rosie O'Day,' 73
  A. saxatilis 'Royal Carpet,' 73
  A. saxatilis 'Silver Queen,' 73
azalea, 60, 66

Baptisia leucantha, 109
basil. *See Ocimum basilicum*
Berberis thunbergii 'Rose Glow' (barberry), 108
Bergenia cordifolia, 26
blue spruce, *8*
bulbs, 26, 60, 66, 88
buttercup, 82
Buxus spp. (boxwood), 88, *110, 117,* 122, 124
  B. sempervirens 'Suffruticosa,' *121,* 122

Calla palustris (hardy calla), 82
Caltha palustris (marsh marigold), 82
Campanula
  C. portenschlagiana, 7
  C. poscharskyana, 7
Campsis spp. (trumpet vine), 32
candytuft. *See Aethionema; Iberis*
cardinal flower. *See Lobelia cardinalis*
Carex (dwarf grass)
  C. 'Bowles Golden,' 91
  C. conica 'Hime Kansuge,' 25, 91
  C. morrowii 'Fisher's Form,' 25
cattails, dwarf. *See Typha minima*
Ceanothus x delilianus 'Gloire de Versailles,' 46-47
Celastrus scandens (American bittersweet), 103

Chamaecyparis obtusa
  C. obtusa 'Nana,' 73
  C. obtusa 'Snowkist,' 73
  C. obtusa 'Spiralis,' 73
chives, 124
chrysanthemum, 25, 87
Clematis spp. 32, 46, 108
  C. 'Candide,' 108
  C. 'Gravetye Beauty,' 116
  C. 'Huldine,' 108
  C. 'Niobe,' 108
  C. paniculata (sweet autumn clematis), 41, *110*
  C. 'Tangutica,' 116
  C. viticella 'Betty Corning,' 116
cobweb houseleek. *See under Sempervivum*
coralbells. *See Heuchera* 'Palace Purple'
Cornus florida 'First Lady,' *3*
Cotinus coggygria 'Royal Purple' (smokebush), 108
cotoneaster, *43*
cranesbill. *See Geranium*
Crataegus viridis 'Winter King,' *121*
crocus, 60
Cyclamen hederifolium, 26
Cyperus
  C. alternifolius (umbrella plant), 83
  C. haspan var. *viviparus* (dwarf papyrus), 83
  C. papyrus (Egyptian paper plant), 83

daffodil, 60
Daphne cneorum, 72
delphinium, 82, 109
Dianthus spp. (pink), 71
Dutchman's-pipe. *See Aristolochia durior*

Echeveria, 72-73
  E. peacockii, 72-73
Echinodorus spp. (sword plant), 83
Eichhornia azurea (purple water hyacinth), 83
Epimedium, 26
  E. 'Niveum,' 26
Erica spp. (heather), 71
Erodium chamaedryoides 'Roseum,' 72

ferns, 7, *65,* 91
  Adiantum pedatum (maidenhair), 7, 66, *89,* 91
  Asplenium scolopendrium (hartstongue), 66
  Athyrium filix-femina (lady), 91
  Athyrium goeringianum 'Pictum' (Japanese painted), 91
  fronds (fiddleheads), 7
  Osmunda cinnamomea (cinnamon), 7
  Osmunda regalis (royal), 7, 91

Polystichum acrostichoides (Christmas), 7, 91
forget-me-not. *See Omphalodes verna*
foxglove, 109
Fremontodendron 'California Glory,' 47

Galium odoratum (sweet woodruff), *57, 60*
gentiana, 71
Geranium (cranesbill), 7, *57,* 72
  G. 'Ballerina,' 60
  G. 'Johnson's Blue,' 7, 60, 108
  G. 'Lancastriense,' 60
  G. sanguineum var. *striatum,* 7, *67, 72*
grape hyacinth, 60
grape vine. *See Vitis* spp.
grasses, 24, 25, 91, *104*
  Carex 'Bowles Golden,' 91
  Carex conica 'Hime Kansuge,' 25, 91
  Carex morrowii 'Fisher's Form,' 25
  Japanese silver, 25
  Miscanthus, 43
  Miscanthus sinensis 'Gracillimus' (maiden), 25
  Ophiopgon planiscapus 'Nigrescens' (dwarf black mondo), 109
  Pennisetum alopecuroides (Rosy fountain), 25

heather. *See Erica* spp.
Hedera spp. (ivy), 7, 32, *39,* 58, *61*
  H. helix 'Thorndale,' 7
Heuchera 'Palace Purple' (coralbells), 109
holly, 25
hollyhock, *23*
honeysuckle. *See Lonicera*
Hosta, 7, 60
  H. 'Blue Wedgewood,' 60
  H. 'Frances Williams,' 7
  H. 'Hadspun Blue,' 60
  H. 'Hadspun Heron,' 60
  H. 'Honeybells,' 116
  H. 'Kabitan,' 60
  H. 'Krossa Regal,' 7
  H. 'Montana,' *57*
  H. 'Royal Standard,' 116
Houttuynia cordata, 91
Humulus japonicus 'Variegatus' (Japanese hops), 103
Hydrangea anomala subsp. *petiolaris* (climbing hydrangea), 32, 41
Hydrocleys nymphoides (water poppy), 83

Iberis (candytuft), *10*
impatiens, 91
Ipomoea spp. (morning-glory), 32, 46
  I. batatas 'Blackie,' 103
  I. 'Heavenly Blue,' 32, *97,* 103, 116
  I. imperialis 'Chocolate,' 103
  I. tricolor, 103

Iris
  I. foetidissima, 26
  I. laevigata (Japanese water iris), 91
  I. laevigata 'Midnight,' 91
  I. laevigata 'Rose Queen,' 91
  I. laevigata 'Snowdrift,' 91
  I. pseudacorus (yellow iris), 82
  I. versicolor (blue iris), 82
ivy. *See Hedera* spp.

Japanese hops. *See Humulus japonicus*
Japanese silver grass, 25
Jasmine. *See Androsace* spp. (rock jasmine); *Trachelospermum jasminoides*
Juniperus communis var. 'Compressa,' 73

Kalanchoe blossfeldiana, 26

lady's-mantle. *See Alchemilla mollis*
lamb's-ears. *See Stachys byzantina*
lantana, 26
Lathyrus odoratus (sweet pea), 32, 103, 116
lemon balm, *43*
lewisia, 71
Lilium vars. (lilies), *23,* 25, 109
liriope, 7, *23,* 25
Lobelia cardinalis (cardinal flower), 82
Lonicera (honeysuckle), 46, 116
  L. 'Dropmore Scarlet,' 46
  L. 'Halliana,' 46
  L. periclymenum var. *belgica,* 116
  L. periclymenum var. *serotina,* 116

Mahonia aquifolium (Oregon grape holly), 26
marjoram, golden. *See Origanum vulgare*
marsh marigold. *See Caltha palustris*
Menispermum canadense (moonseed), 41
Miscanthus, 43
  M. sinensis 'Gracillimus' (maiden grass), 25
morning-glory. *See Ipomoea* spp.
moss campion. *See Silene acaulis*

Nymphaea spp. (water lily), 83-84
  N. odorata, 83
  N. tuberosa, 83
Nymphoides indica (water snowflake), 83

Ocimum basilicum (basil), 124
Omphalodes verna (forget-me-not), *65,* 124
Ophiopogon planiscapus 'Nigrescens' (dwarf black mondo grass), 109
Oregon grape holly. *See Mahonia aquifolium*
Origanum vulgare 'Aureum' (golden marjoram), 124
Osmunda
  O. cinnamomea (cinnamon fern), 7

O. regalis (royal fern), 7, 91

pachysandra, *3,* 7, 58
papyrus/paper plant. *See under Cyperus*
peony, *10*
parsley, 124
Pennisetum alopecuroides (Rosy fountain grass), 25
Picea abies 'Little Gem,' 73
Polystichum acrostichoides (Christmas fern), 7, 91
Pontederia cordata (pickerel rush), 82-83
porcelain vine. *See Ampelopsis brevipendunculata*
Potentilla
  P. 'Miss Wilmott,' *8*
  P. verna 'Nana,' 72
prairie verbena. *See Verbena rigida*
Primula, 66
  P. modesta, 72
Prunus subhirtella 'Pendula' (weeping cherry), *20*

quince, *110*

rock cress. *See Arabis* spp.
rock jasmine. *See Androsace* spp.
Rosa (rose), *29,* 30, 32, 34-37, 53, 88, *92,* 116, *117,* 122-24
  R. 'Aimée Vibert,' 54
  R. 'Albertine,' *33*
  R. 'Alchymist,' 37, *121,* 123
  R. 'Aloha,' 37
  R. 'America,' 54
  R. banksiae alba plena, 37
  R. banksiae 'Lutea' (Lady Banks Rose), 37
  R. 'Baroness Rothschild,' *49, 120, 121,* 122, 123
  R. 'Belle Isis,' *120,* 123
  R. 'Boule de Neige,' *120, 121,* 122
  R. 'Bullata,' (Lettuce Leaf Rose), *121,* 124
  R. 'Cardinal de Richelieu,' *121,* 123
  R. 'Climbing Crimson Glory,' 54
  R. 'Comte de Chambord,' *120,* 122
  R. 'Constance Spry,' 54, *121,* 123
  R. 'David Thompson,' *39*
  R. 'Dr. Van Fleet,' 37
  R. 'Don Juan,' 37
  R. 'Fantin Latour,' *120,* 122
  R. 'Félicité et Perpétue,' 54
  R. gallica officinalis (Apothecary Rose), *120,* 122
  R. 'Golden Showers,' 54, 116
  R. 'Golden Wings,' *120,* 122
  R. 'Goldrush,' 37
  R. 'Gruss an Aachen,' *120,* 123
  R. 'Heritage,' *120,* 123
  R. 'Léda,' *120,* 122
  R. 'Leontyne Gervais,' 54

R. 'Lilian Austin,' *120*, 122
R. 'Madame Alfred Carrière,' *34*, 54
R. 'May Queen,' 54
R. 'New Dawn,' 37
R. 'Parkdirector Riggers,' 54
R. 'Royal Sunset,' 54
R. rubrifolia (R. glauca), 40
R. 'Tuscany,' *120, 121*, 123
R. 'Tuscany Superb,' 123
R. 'White Bath' *(R. centifolia muscosa alba), 121*, 123
R. 'White Dawn,' 37
R. 'Yellow Rambler,' *34*, 37
R. 'Zéphirine Drouhin,' 108, *120*, 122-23
rosemary, 26
Russian sage, *8*

Sagittaria spp. (arrowhead), 82
　S. 'Florepleno,' 82
　S. latifolia, 82
sand verbena. *See Abronia* spp.
santolina, 26
saxifrage, 26, 72
　Kabschia, 71
Sedum, 72, 73
　S. dasyphyllum (stonecrop), *67*
Sempervivum, 72, 73
　S. arachnoideum (cobweb houseleek), 73
Silene acaulis (moss campion), 72
smokebush. *See Cotinus coggygria* 'Royal Purple'
snowdrops, 26, 60
Stachys byzantina (lamb's-ears), 7, *110*, 124
　'Silver Carpet,' 7, 109
sweet flag. *See Acorus*
sweet pea. *See Lathyrus odoratus*
sweet woodruff. *See Galium odoratum*
sword plant. *See Echinodorus* spp.

thrift. *See Armeria* spp.
Thymus (thyme), 73
　T. serpyllum (mother-of-thyme), 72
　T. x citriodorus 'Aureus,' 124
Trachelospermum jasminoides (jasmine), 46
　T. jasminoides 'Madison,' 46
trumpet vine. *See Campsis* spp.
Tsuga canadensis 'Pygmaea,' 73
Typha minima (dwarf cattails), 82

umbrella plant. *See under Cyperus*

Verbena rigida (prairie verbena), 26
veronica, 72
vinca, 58
Viburnum plicatum 'Mariesii,' 108
Vitis spp. (grape vine), *110*, 116
　V. 'Cardinal,' 116
　V. 'Interlaken,' 116
　V. 'Thompson Seedless,' 116

water hyacinth, purple. *See Eichhornia azurea*
water lily. *See Nymphaea* spp.
water poppy. *See Hydrocleys nymphoides*
water snowflake. *See Nymphoides indica*
weeping cherry. *See Prunus subhirtella* 'Pendula'
wisteria, 30, 116

Yucca, 67
　Y. filamentosa, 108

Zinnia, 23
　Z. grandiflora (Rocky Mountain zinnia), 26